The
Long Ride
Home

Other Books in the Keystone Stables series

The Long Ride Home

BOOK 8

KEYSTONE
Stables

..... Marsha Hubler .....

ZONDERkidz

ZONDERVAN.com/
AUTHORTRACKER
follow your favorite authors

We want to hear from you. Please send your comments
about this book to us in care of zreview@zondervan.com. Thank you.

ZONDERKIDZ

The Long Ride Home
Copyright © 2009 by Marsha Hubler

Requests for information should be addressed to:
Zonderkidz, *Grand Rapids, MI 49530*

Library of Congress Cataloging-in-Publication Data

Hubler, Marsha, 1947-
    The long ride home / by Marsha Hubler.
        p. cm. — (Keystone Stables ; bk. 8)
    Summary: Thirteen-year-old Skye, who lives at Keystone Stables with her
foster parents and wheelchair-bound foster sister, has been wondering about
her real parents, and, with God's help, she is finally able to meet them.
    ISBN 978-0-310-71692-1 (softcover)
    [1. Foster home care—Fiction. 2. Parents—Fiction. 3. Horses—Fiction.
4. People with disabilities—Fiction. 5. Christian life—Fiction.] I. Title.
    PZ7.H86325 Lo 2010
    [Fic]—dc22   2009033133

Interior illustrator: Lyn Boyer
Interior design and composition: Carlos Estrada and Sherri L. Hoffman

Printed in the United States of America

13 14 15 16 /DCI/ 23 22 21 20 19 18 17 16 15 14 13 12 11 10 9 8 7 6 5 4

Dedicated to all my foster children,
whom I love as my own.

chapter one

The waitress carrying two coffee pots walked to the table and stood beside Mr. Chambers. "More coffee, sir?"

Skye glanced at the waitress, who stared back with a strange look on her face.

"Regular, please," Mr. Chambers said, handing the waitress his cup.

The waitress poured the coffee, shifting her glance from Mr. Chambers' cup to Skye and back. The waitress's dark hair, the color of Skye's, was drawn back into a ponytail and adorned by a yellow cap that daintily covered her crown. In a blue top, black pants and a frilly yellow apron, the petite woman, probably in her early thirties, looked like she needed a good dose of vitamins. On her apron bib a small silver nametag displayed her name: MILLIE.

"How about you, ma'am?" Millie asked Mrs. Chambers, now with a slight edge to her voice. The waitress never took her eyes off Skye.

"No thank you," Mrs. Chambers said. "I'm fine."

Walking away, the waitress glanced back at Skye one more time.

"Mom," Skye said, "did you see how that waitress stared at me?"

"Sure did," Mrs. Chambers said. "You probably remind her of someone she knows. That often happens to me. I can be hundreds of miles away from home, but, almost without fail, I'll see a stranger who looks like someone I know."

"Been there, done that, too," Morgan agreed.

Skye pulled her focus away from Millie and studied her surroundings. "This place is too cool," she said. In a diner on the outskirts of Charleston, South Carolina, she was about to enjoy a Saturday evening meal of burgers and fries with her foster parents, Tom and Eileen Chambers, and her foster sister, fifteen-year-old Morgan Hendricks, who sat in a wheelchair. In the diner's parking lot, their horse trailer was hosting an oats-and-hay feast for the family's four show horses, including Skye's pride and joy, her sorrel Quarter Horse Champ.

Back at Keystone Stables, Skye's good friend Chad Dressler was house-sitting, looking after the two Westies, Tippy Canoe and Tyler Too, as well as the family's two other horses.

After spending the last week of June at a state horse show in Virginia, the Chambers' family was now heading to Rebucks' Rocking Horse Ranch, a Christian special-needs dude ranch in the southeast corner of South Carolina near Charleston. As short-term staff, they would donate their time there for the next two weeks. Morgan planned to work in the kitchen while Mr. Chambers would volunteer his carpentry skills to remodel the chapel. Mrs. Chambers and Skye would teach horse care and Western riding techniques to about a hundred campers. On some of their time off, they planned to visit Mr. Chambers' sister, Dot, who lived in North Charleston.

As the Chambers family settled at a table, Skye studied the unique décor of the "Cozy Cupboard." Reminiscent of the 50s, the small diner oozed with mouth-watering smells and delicious-looking food. At the counter, a row of tired men, truck drivers Skye figured, had lined up on the stools to grab a quick bite. Along one windowed wall a row of booths held numerous patrons who talked as slowly as they ate. Between the counter and booths most of the tables were occupied, one of them with the Chambers clan. The floor, in gray and red tile blocks, displayed an original design of scuffmarks and food stains. One waitress behind the counter and two others moving through the dining room had barely enough time to breathe as they hustled with orders, trying their best to exude a pleasant demeanor. In the background, country music blared.

Within minutes the Chambers' food was served, Mr. Chambers prayed, and the family's conversation focused on the past week's activities.

"Girls, I can't begin to tell you how proud I am of you." Mr. Chambers took a sip of his coffee and smoothed his brown mustache. "We're taking home seven blue ribbons and five red ones, and most of them are yours."

Skye's brown eyes flashed as she tucked her long dark hair behind her ears. "I started to lose count about halfway through the week. Dad, you didn't do too bad yourself. When you won first place in calf roping, you and Chief broke your own time, didn't you?"

"By a half second." Mr. Chambers replied proudly. "That little Paint cowpony of mine can really fly. And how about the woman of the house and Pepsi?" He gave Mrs. Chambers a quick wink. "They cleaned up the Western Reining Class. I don't think they could have done any better with a vacuum cleaner."

Mrs. Chambers' deep blue eyes sparkled as she smiled at her husband. "Oh, Tom, stop that carrying on. I had an easier time this year because the competition was not as keen as in the past. But Pepsi *was* at the top of her game. I will agree with that." She shifted her glance across the table to Morgan. "And how about our special-needs gal, here? She and Blaze *blazed* up a storm in their barrel-racing event too. Second place out of ten in a regional championship is nothing to sneeze at."

Morgan's freckled face beamed with her usual radiant smile. Her sunburned cheeks matched the color of her long wavy red hair. "Thanks, Mrs. C.," she said, blowing on her fingernails. "I guess when you've got it, you've got it!"

"Girls, are you ready for next week?" Mr. Chambers asked, taking a bite of his double burger.

"Dad," Skye said, "I'm so excited, I can't stand it." She shoved a French fry in her mouth. "I never thought serving the Lord could be like this. I mean, Champ and I will be serving the Lord together. How cool is that?"

"Although I can't *stand it* anytime in this wheelchair, I'm going bonkers too," Morgan said, giggling. "I can't wait to get in that camp kitchen to peel hard-boiled eggs and potatoes. I know that sounds weird for a teenager, but I love every part of cooking, even stuff like that. I can't believe that we'll all be doing things we love so much."

"That's the way God works," Mr. Chambers said. "It says in Proverbs that he'll give us the desires of our heart if we love him and trust him. He's proven himself over and over to us."

"Skye, will you — " Mrs. Chambers started to say.

Crash!

Passing close to the Chambers' table, Millie dropped a full tray of food onto the hard tile floor. Spaghetti and meatballs flew everywhere, and the vintage Melmac dishes bounced off the tile floor like rubber balls, sending an irritating echo through the entire place. Skye jumped like she'd been poked with a pin. Everyone turned and stared, and the place grew dead silent.

"I am so sorry." Millie was already on her knees, trying her best to clean up the mess.

"Accidents do happen." Mr. Chambers, his clothes littered with red blotches, shoved back his chair and picked up several plastic glasses.

Mrs. Chambers and Skye launched out of their chairs and brushed off spaghetti from their clothes. From a swinging door behind the counter, a man in a chef's hat, blue shirt, and white apron came rushing out. He lugged a large bucket of soapy water, a mop, and another bucket that was empty. "You got butter fingers tonight, Millie?" the man said gruffly as he pitched in.

"I'm sorry, Butch," Millie said, shoving spilled food and plates into the empty bucket. "It was a little heavy."

"We'll have to put you on steroids," Butch said as though he meant it. "I'm terribly sorry folks," he said to Mr. Chambers. "Your meals are on the house."

"It's all right," Mr. Chambers said as he helped Millie. "Nobody's hurt. That's what matters."

Skye looked around, and except for two small children still gawking, everyone else had gone back to their meals as though nothing had happened. She glanced under the table and saw a biscuit near Morgan's foot. Quickly, she retrieved the roll and placed it in the trash bucket.

"Thank you," Millie said as she, again, stared briefly at Skye and resumed her clean-up job.

Butch finished wiping the floor and hurried away. "Remember, folks," he yelled back without looking, "the meals are on me tonight. Millie, a fresh order of what you just dropped will be ready in ten."

"Thanks, Butch," Millie said. "Be there in a sec."

While Morgan supplied clean napkins from the table's dispenser, Mr. and Mrs. Chambers and Skye worked at wiping spots from their clothes. Finally, after a quick sweep of their chairs, they sat down to finish their meal.

Millie stood beside Skye, grabbed an array of soiled napkins from the table, and stuffed them in her apron pocket. "Folks," she said sheepishly, "I apologize again for scaring you out of your wits." She fingered her collar, crossed her arms, then placed her hands on her hips, all the while staring at Skye.

Mr. Chambers held up his hand. "Now, that's all right. No harm done."

"No, really," Millie said, fidgeting with her collar again. "I was startled when I heard someone here call this young lady 'Skye.'"

Skye glanced at Mom and Dad Chambers' surprised faces. With her mind full of questions, Skye looked deep into Millie's brown eyes. "Do ... you ... know me?" she asked.

"I think I do," Millie said. "Is your name Skye Nicholson?"

chapter two

really can't talk now," Millie said, glancing at her watch. "I get off in a half hour. If we can meet then, I'll explain everything."

Skye sat with her mouth stuck in neutral.

"By all means," Mr. Chambers said. "We'll be waiting right here."

"Could I meet you outside in back of the restaurant?" Millie asked, eyes focused intensely on Skye. "There's a picnic table there where us waitresses go for breaks."

"Sure, that'll be fine," Mrs. Chambers said.

What's going on? Skye wondered.

"In a half hour then?" Millie smiled at Skye, turned, and hurried away.

"In a half hour," Mr. Chambers yelled after her.

As Millie rush behind the counter to pick up her next order, Skye watched every move the woman made. "Mom, who is she?"

"Other than her name being Millie, I have no idea," Mrs. Chambers said.

"And, Skye, how does she know your last name?" Morgan asked.

"These are questions we soon should have answered," Mr. Chambers said. "Let's finish our meals and we'll check on the horses before we meet with this woman, whoever she is."

"I can't eat now," Skye moaned. "I feel sick." She put down her fork and stared at Millie. "Do you think she's my real mother?"

Mrs. Chambers reached across the table and touched Skye's arm. "Honey, we'll find out soon enough. You know, I'm not so hungry myself."

Who is Millie and what does this all mean? Skye's unanswered questions tumbled in her brain like leaves in a whirlwind as the Chambers' table exuded an uncommon silence. Skye stared at her foster mother, whose forced smile betrayed a deep worry. Skye glanced at her foster dad and then Morgan, who both wore similar looks that reflected exactly how Skye was feeling inside.

Skye took a quick glance at Millie and then back to her foster parents, who had taken her in and had loved her through all her troubles and trials. Again, she looked at Morgan, who looked more worried and distant than ever before. Morgan never worried about anything.

Suddenly, Skye wasn't quite sure if she even wanted to know who this Millie person was. In a half hour, Skye reasoned, her world as she knew it could shatter like an old glass bottle from a shotgun blast. Was she ready to face such overwhelming insecurity that suddenly lay blocking her life's path? With a sigh, she realized she had no choice. The unknown was coming for her, and she could do nothing to stop it.

At the picnic table behind the diner, Skye stood up and glanced at her watch. "It's been thirty-five minutes. Maybe she left."

"I don't think so," Mr. Chambers said. "She's got something to tell us, Skye, and I think, whatever it is, it's very important."

"The suspense is killing me." Even with her worried look, Morgan tried to lighten the mood. "I just wonder how she knows your name."

The door of the diner opened, and out rushed Millie, carrying a bulging red wallet that had seen better days. She hurried to the table and stared at Skye.

"How do you know me?" Skye stood behind Mrs. Chambers and put her hands firmly on her foster mother's shoulders.

Millie took a deep breath as she glanced around the table, and her eyes suddenly teared up. With jittery hands, she opened her wallet and pulled out a packet of folded papers and cards. She nervously shuffled through them and separated what looked like a photo from the pile. "Skye, is your birthday January 15th and are you thirteen years old?" Millie's voice quivered uncontrollably.

"Y-yes," Skye barely managed to say. "Are … are you my real mother?"

Millie handed the photo to Mrs. Chambers. "This is me holding Skye eleven years ago." Pulling a shriveled-up tissue from her apron pocket, she dabbed her eyes, red and now flooding with tears. "Skye, I'm Millie Nicholson Eister. I'm your aunt. Your father is my brother."

Skye's entire body quivered as she stared at the picture that showed a younger Millie, not much thinner than she was now, holding a toddler with dark brown hair and brown eyes very much like Skye's. Skye's knees wobbled, and she was certain that any passing breeze would topple her right over. She tightened her grip on her foster mother's shoulders, and Mrs. Chambers reached up and firmly grasped her one hand. Skye glanced at Morgan and Mr. Chambers, whose faces both mirrored Skye's emotional turmoil.

"But—how?" Skye rambled. "Where's my father? Who is he? And where's my mother?"

"Millie, please sit down." Mr. Chambers gestured, then nervously stroked his mustache. "I'm sure you have a lot to tell us."

Mrs. Chambers handed the photo to her husband, who studied it carefully and showed it to Morgan. Millie edged herself onto the bench across from Mrs. Chambers.

"I'm sure this is a big shock to all of you." Millie dabbed tears from her eyes. "I can hardly believe it myself. I've been wondering what happened to Skye all these years after she went into foster care. No matter how hard I tried, I never could find out a thing about her from the agencies. I had pretty much given up hope."

"But—where are my parents?" Skye's voice quivered.

"Easy, Skye," Mrs. Chambers said, squeezing her hand tighter. "We'll find out in good time."

"I don't even know where to start," Millie said.

"Start at the beginning," Mr. Chambers said. "Just take your time."

"Yeah, we have all night." Morgan's words seemed forced. "This is a super moment for Skye."

Again, Mrs. Chambers squeezed Skye's hand. "Honey, sit down, and let's hear what Millie has to say."

Skye slipped next to her foster mom, folding her hands to keep them from shaking. With her mind exploding with questions, she could do nothing but stare at Millie Nicholson Eister, a perfect stranger, her aunt.

Millie took a deep breath and began. "Skye, your father's name is Jacy Nicholson. We grew up in Pittsburgh."

"His name is Jacy?" Skye asked.

"Yes," Millie answered. "He was named after our father—your grandfather—James Collier Nicholson. Our parents used the initials J. and C. and gave him the name Jacy. By the way, when you were born, you were the spittin' image of your dad. You were his pride and joy."

16

"You grew up in Pittsburgh, Pennsylvania?" Morgan said. "We live in Pennsylvania now."

"I figured you were from the north somewhere," Millie said a half smile. "No southern drawl. Anyway, after Jacy graduated from a tech school, he worked as a mechanic at a garage on the outskirts of southern Pittsburgh. A few years later, he married his childhood sweetheart, Rita Ulmer."

"My mother's name is Rita?" Skye asked. "Where is she?"

Mrs. Chambers patted Skye's hands. "Just wait, honey. You'll find out."

"At first their marriage was a happy one, especially after they had you. You were their only child. But Jacy started running with some men who drank, so he started hitting the bottle too. That's when things went terribly wrong." Again, Millie dabbed at the tears making wet tracks down both sides of her face. "Eleven years ago, Jacy and Rita were in a horrible accident. Jacy was speeding and went head-on into another car. Although Jacy and Rita were only banged up a little, the other driver, a young mother of two small children, was killed."

"Oh, my," Mrs. Chambers gasped, her hand covering her mouth.

"That must have been awful," Skye said.

Millie continued. "Rita never drank much in her younger years, but that night she was loaded, too, and resisted arrest. To spare herself from jail time, she testified against Jacy in court. He was convicted of vehicular homicide and was sentenced to fifteen years at one of the state pens."

"Is he still there?" Skye asked. "Where is the prison? And where's my mother?"

"Skye, let her finish," Dad Chambers chided softly.

Millie sniffled, pulled out another tissue from her pocket and blew her nose. "I'm afraid the story doesn't get any better."

"Tell us everything you know," Mrs. Chambers pleaded. "Skye has always wanted to know about her parents. I believe God brought you into our lives at this time so she can have some closure."

"When Rita testified against my brother, he swore he'd get even with her. After the judge handed down the sentence and they were dragging him out of court, he yelled that when he'd get out of jail, he'd find her and kill her. She was so scared, she took drastic measures so he'd never find her."

"Drastic measures?" Mrs. Chambers asked.

Another barrage of tears flowed freely down the woman's face. "With the help of the police, Rita changed her whole identity. She divorced Jacy and quit her job. Skye, although it broke her heart, she left you with me. She thought that as a single woman, she could hide out somewhere in another part of the country better than someone with a small child."

"If you had me, then how did I get into foster care?" Skye asked.

"This is so hard." The Chambers family waited silently as Millie sobbed. "I was a single mother with two kids of my own," Millie continued. "I just didn't have the means to keep you. That's when I placed you in foster care." Through her tears, she smiled at Skye. "It looks like you've got a real good home now, and that makes me so happy."

"How did you get down here in the Charleston area?" Mr. Chambers asked.

"Jacy was the only family I had," Millie said. "My marriage had just broken up, and when Jacy was sent up, he wrote me out of his life because I helped Rita and then had to give up Skye. So, I decided to move down here and start all over. I thought me and my two kids could make a go of it down here. I had no idea what happened to Skye after the agency came to pick her up all those years ago."

"But what about my mother?" Skye asked. "Where is she now? And how can I get in touch with her and my father?"

Millie took a deep jagged breath and sighed. "I'm—I'm afraid ..." She lowered her head onto her arms and sobbed uncontrollably.

"Are they dead?" Skye's voice screeched with panic. "They are, aren't they? I know they are!"

Millie finally managed to regain her composure. She lifted her head and wiped her face with a steady supply of tissues from Mrs. Chambers. Millie took a deep, jagged breath and made a desperate effort to smile through her next few words. "Skye, I just don't know—about either of them. Your dad was sentenced to serve his time at the Brentwood State Penitentiary about forty miles south of Pittsburgh. When I tried to visit him, he wouldn't see me. I wrote him every week for months, but he never responded. Another inmate who knew Jacy had written to me and said that Jacy was very angry at me and Rita, really at the whole world, and he pretty much kept to himself. I wrote to this other inmate several times—his name was Charlie Hamlock. He wrote back for a while, but then he stopped. As far as I know your dad is still at that same pen."

"Did you ever hear from Skye's mother again?" Mr. Chambers asked.

efore Rita left town," Millie said between sniffles, "she destroyed all evidence of her former life. She even went through my house and took all the pictures of her family and trashed them. Thank the dear Lord she didn't check my wallet. She never told me her new name or contacted me after she left." Millie pointed to the beat-up photo on the table. "That's all I have left of her—and of you, Skye. I've held that picture close to my heart all these years. I've often just sat and stared at that picture and wondered where you were. I can't tell you how I feel right now. Seeing you after all these years is—is—like a miracle." Millie's face lit up, revealing a set of teeth that needed more than one visit to the dentist. It was the first sincere smile Skye had seen on the woman.

Skye's glance darted from Millie to Mrs. Chambers. "Mom, how can we find out if my father's still at that prison? Can't we call and ask?"

"I'm afraid not," Mrs. Chambers said. "The prisons won't release any information about their inmates to just anybody. They won't even tell us if he's been released or not."

"Then how can we find out?" Morgan asked.

"Yeah, how?" Skye added.

"We'll go online to a website called 'Department of Corrections.' Believe it or not, if he's in a prison anywhere in the U.S., we'll be able to find out."

"Heaven knows, I've tried to call Jacy and write over all these years, but it was no use." Millie wiped her nose again. "I never thought of going on the Internet to see where he is now."

"I'm a counselor of troubled youth at the Maranatha Treatment Center in central PA," Mrs. Chambers said. "On numerous occasions I've tried to track someone down, either a missing client or someone's relative."

"We have our laptop with us," Skye piped in. "Let's look for my dad right now."

"Easy, girl," Mr. Chambers said. "All in good time."

"Several of our past foster kids have needed information about someone in prison too," Mrs. Chambers added. "We've been able to help one or two with the Internet."

"Hmm," Millie said, "that's amazing. It's too bad we don't know Rita's new name. I bet we could find her on the Internet, too."

"Probably so," Mrs. Chambers said.

"Can't we check online now? I'll go get the laptop." By now, Skye was desperate.

"Wait a minute, honey." Mrs. Chambers gently tapped Skye's hand. "Over the next twenty-four hours we have to arrive at camp, get the horses bedded down, move into our family quarters, and report for orientation. Our heads will be spinning."

"But I can't wait that long. I'll just die!" Skye chewed her lip and glanced around the table, focusing on Morgan, who sat strangely quiet with no expression on her face. *That's so not like her,* Skye thought. *She's usually upbeat about everything.*

"And, Skye, somewhere in between we have to eat again ... not to mention sleep," Mr. Chambers said.

Millie picked up the photo of Skye as though it were made of glass. "I'm sure you'd like a copy of this, so I'll get one made ASAP. Now, you mentioned that you're staying at a camp. How can I keep in touch?"

"We'll give you our cell phone number," Mr. Chambers said. "For the next two weeks, we'll be working at Rebucks' Rocking Horse Ranch on the shore side of Charleston. We've just come from a week-long horse show in Virginia—"

"Skye and her horse, Champ, won four blue ribbons!" Morgan interjected. "You should see her ride!"

That's the Morgan I know. Skye reasoned, then directed her words at Millie. "Don't you have any information at all about my mother?"

"I'm afraid not," Millie said. "She's been in hiding a long time."

"Would you be able to come visit us sometime in Pennsylvania?" Skye asked.

"I'd like that very much." Millie's watery eyes sparkled with a newfound hope. "My two kids and I would love to be able to say we have family other than just the three of us."

"What are my cousins' names?" Skye asked.

"Yes," Mrs. Chambers said, "please tell us all about them—and you yourself."

Millie smiled again, this time glowing with obvious pride. She pulled two more photos from her wallet and handed them to Skye. "This is Dennis. He's nineteen and he just joined the Marines. He's stationed in Norfolk at the naval base. He's in supply, you know, making sure the troops have enough ammo, gear, that kind of thing. My daughter's name is Emma, and she's seventeen. She's always on the honor roll, and this summer she's working

22

two part-time jobs to earn money for college next year. I've always wanted my kids to have things better than me."

"It looks like you've done a pretty decent job," Mr. Chambers said.

"Wow," Skye said, "Emma is really pretty. I can't believe I'm actually looking at my real, living, breathing true-to-life cousin."

Mrs. Chambers leaned toward Skye and stared at the photo. "And I see she has dark hair and brown eyes like you, Skye. There's definitely a family resemblance."

"Gorgeous, of course," Skye kidded and handed the photos to Morgan. "What do you think?" she said with a giggle.

"Well," Morgan said as she studied the pictures, "Emma and you do kinda look alike. Gorgeous, of course! And Private Dennis Eister is one handsome dude in his dress blues."

"Uniforms seem to run in my family," Millie said. "One of Emma's jobs is at a fast-food joint. She really looks cute in maroon and gold. The other job she has is in a toy store at a mall. Although there's no uniform there, she loves that job because she loves kids. She wants to be a teacher."

Mr. Chambers studied the pictures intently. "We'll have to try to arrange to meet your family, Millie. We'd like to get to know you all better."

"Well, Denny won't have leave until the end of the summer," Millie said, "but Emma still lives at home. I know where the Rebuck camp is. Since you're going to be in the Charleston area for two weeks, I'd love to see Skye, really all of you, again."

"And we can meet Emma," Skye added.

"I'll tell you one thing," Millie said with another broad smile. "I'm going to knock Emma's socks off with this news. I've told her all about Skye since Emma was old enough to understand. She'll be thrilled to pieces to meet her only cousin."

Mr. Chambers handed the two photos back to Millie. "Well, let's definitely plan on getting together again. Once we're settled at the camp, we'll call you."

"I'll be waiting," Millie said with a chuckle. "I'll tie my cell phone around my neck."

"And Skye," Mr. Chambers said. "The first chance we get, we'll check the Internet. We want to find your father as much as you do."

chapter four

The first chance Skye had to go online was Sunday after camp chapel and lunch when the teen volunteer staff finally had some free time. While Mr. and Mrs. Chambers attended an orientation class, Skye and Morgan went to their cabin, turned on the computer, and started their search.

As they began, Morgan stared straight at Skye to ask her a question. "Skye, why are you so gung ho to find your parents?"

"Why wouldn't I be?" Skye blurted out, almost stunned by Morgan's question. Light-hearted Morgan seemed deeply troubled—by something. Skye's thoughts quickly transported her to the first day she had met Morgan at Keystone Stables. Ever since then they had been best friends, as close as sisters. But now Skye felt a strange distance between them, and she needed to find out why. She leaned back in her chair and looked into Morgan's eyes. "Morgan, what's the matter with you? I've noticed you've been acting kinda funny."

"I just want to know why you want to find your parents. That's all," Morgan said.

"I've always wanted to find them," Skye said. "You know that. Does it bother you?"

"Nah, not really. You just seem like you're in your own little world lately."

"Well, I'll try to come back to earth," Skye giggled. "I'll put it in writing, if you want." Skye giggled as she found the Department of Corrections website and plugged in her father's name. After several attempts, she came up dry. Skye had run into her first wall, and it was solid stone.

"Hey," Morgan suggested, "try Family and Friend Search. Some of the kids in our youth group said that website promises to 'find anyone across the entire USA.' I've been thinking of plugging my dad's name in, but I haven't done it yet."

Skye went to the website but also got nowhere. Fourteen men with the name "Jacy Nicholson" were listed, their addresses scattered all over the country, and she had no idea where to begin.

"Sally, easy on the reins now," Skye said on Monday morning in the training corral at the Rebucks' Rocking Horse Ranch. The air was so steamy hot, she could have sworn she heard it hissing around her as she tackled her first assignment instructing a beginning rider.

Standing in the center, Skye worked Champ on a longeing line. Obediently, he circled the ring in a slow trot, carrying an eight-year-old girl with Down syndrome who was doing her best to listen to Skye's instructions.

"Keep your heels close to his belly," Skye said, "and your toes pointed out. That's good, Sally, very good."

Ordinarily, Skye would be one hundred percent into a job like this one. Working with kids and horses was right up her alley, and she was determined to do the best job she possibly could. But her thoughts drifted constantly to Millie and what the woman had said about Skye's father and mother. So although Skye did her job, and did it well, she just couldn't keep her mind from drifting back over the last day-and-a-half's events.

So much has happened since Friday at that diner! How am I ever going to find the right Jacy Nicholson? Maybe he's not even using that name anymore. Maybe he's in another country. Maybe he's dead! And where's my mother? What's her name now? Skye's mind darted from Sally to Millie and churned like tumbleweed in a dust storm as she tried to decide what to do next to find her parents. Finally, she forced herself back to her work with Sally and Champ in the riding ring.

"Okay, Sally!" Skye said to her young student. "Pull gently on the reins and make Champ stop. The riding part of your lesson is over for today." Skye approached Sally still sitting on Champ and looped the longeing line in her hands. Removing the line from Champ's halter, Skye patted Champ's sweaty neck. "Good boy, Champ," she said, and then looked at Sally.

Sally's hardhat and long blonde curls framed plump rosy cheeks and brown puppy-dog eyes with curly lashes. "How'd I do, Skye? Did I keep my feet turned right? I wasn't pulling too hard on his reins, was I? I just love Champy," she went on, "and I want a horse just like him when I get big. Where can I get one just like him?"

Skye giggled to herself. *"At a loss for words" will certainly never be this cutie's motto.* "Sally, you did just fine for your first lesson. We have all week to talk about how you can get your own horse when you are all grown up. The next thing you need to learn is how to take off the saddle and bridle and how to groom him. Horses love to be brushed. Are you ready to do that?"

"Oh, yes," Sally said. "Where do we do that? Can we do that now, Skye?"

"We sure can," Skye said. She grabbed Champ's cheek strap and turned him toward the barn. "Sally, we'll walk Champ to the door. There I'll help you dismount, and then we'll take off his tack and you can groom him."

"Oh, this is so cool," Sally bubbled. "I've never even been on a horse before, and now I get to brush one and everything!"

"I'll show you how to comb his mane and tail, too. Let's go."

Just as Skye led Champ to a hitching post in front of the barn, she spotted her foster mother coming toward her from the direction of the administration office. Dressed in her tan and red western riding clothes, Mrs. Chambers made a stunning appearance. Even in the shade of her tan Stetson, her blue eyes sparkled.

"Hi, Mom," Skye said, "What's up? I thought our trail ride didn't start until after lunch."

Mrs. Chambers folded her arms on the top rail of the fence. "It doesn't," she said. "But I—"

"Ooh, a trail ride," Sally blurted out. "Can I go on that, Skye, can I, huh?"

"I'm afraid not," Skye said. "That's for the older kids. But you'll get to ride here tomorrow morning in the corral again."

"Oh, okay," Sally said. "Can I get down now?"

"Sure you can," Skye said and then turned. "One moment, Mom." Skye held her index finger up toward Mrs. Chambers and then tied Champ to the post.

Skye reached up and slid Sally out of the saddle. "Now just wait one second until this nice lady and I talk about something, okay?"

"Okay," Sally said.

"Now stand here in front of Champ and pet him on the nose." Skye reached into her jeans pocket and pulled out three sugar cubes. "Give him these. And hold one at

28

a time with your hand flat like this. Then he'll be able to nibble it without biting you."

"Okay." Sally started to follow Skye's instructions.

Watching Sally carefully, Skye stepped to the fence where Mrs. Chambers waited. "What's happening?" Skye asked.

"Well, I just had a phone call from Millie, and I'm wondering if you'd like to skip the trail ride. Millie and Emma don't have to work this afternoon, and they want to come here to see you." Mrs. Chambers pointed her thumb over her shoulder. "The office said they can have one of their hired help cover for you, if you'd like. I'm on my way to the barn to groom the horses and get them ready for the ride."

For the first time in Skye's life since she had met Champ, she had to decide whether she wanted to do something else rather than be with her beloved horse. But, as she had correctly assumed when she met Millie, things in her life would probably change, and the changes had already begun.

Skye glanced back at Champ and quickly analyzed the situation. In the blink of an eye, she had acquired "family," not that the Chambers and Morgan weren't, but Millie and her two kids were "real family," the one she longed to know. She simply had to find out more.

"What time can they be here?" Skye said with a racing heart.

chapter five

At one o'clock, Skye sat at a center table in the empty mess hall waiting for Millie and Emma. From behind the serving counter busy voices, rattling glasses, and clanging pots echoed throughout the entire hall. A heavy garlic smell from a lasagna lunch still saturated the spacious room, but Skye was so focused on Millie's arrival, the commotion and smells seemed miles away.

Skye sat so that she could observe both entrance doors on opposite sides of the cafeteria. The door to her left swung open, and Skye stared in that direction, her heart taking a funny beat. Two teen boys wearing white aprons hurried inside and then headed into the kitchen.

Skye glanced at her watch and sighed. *Five after one. Millie said they'd be here around one. That could mean one thirty—or one forty five!* She sipped a glass half full of warm lemonade, raked her fingers through her hair, and tapped her fingernails on the table. *Where are they?*

The door to her right swung open and in came Millie, followed by a teen girl who could easily pass for Skye's sister. Clutching her red wallet and keys, Millie had on her waitress uniform, minus the cap, and Emma wore an orange tank top and jean shorts. In Emma's arms was a humongous book with a blue-flowered cloth and white lace cover. *Her hair is exactly like mine,* Skye thought. *The same color and length and everything. This is too cool.*

Skye smiled and stood as both visitors smiled back and headed toward the center of the room.

That big book's gotta be a photo album, Skye surmised.

Skye was never much into hugging, but she suddenly had a strange urge to do so. After all, this was her real family, and real families were supposed to hug. She chewed her bottom lip and contemplated what to do. *They might not be into hugging either,* she reasoned and, although she wanted to run into Millie's arms, Skye held back and waited.

"Skye, honey, how are you?" Millie blurted out and gave Skye a warm embrace. "Let me look at you," she said as she moved Skye to arm's length and their eyes met. "I still can't believe you're Jacy's little girl, all grown up — and standing right before my very eyes."

"I'm fine — ah — Aunt Millie," Skye said. Without warning, tears blurred her vision as she glanced at Emma. "Let me guess," Skye joked. "Could this be Cousin Emma?"

"Hi," Emma said, her voice quivering with excitement. "I've heard so much about you, I feel like I already know you. I almost went nuts when Mom told me what happened at the diner Friday night. She's been telling me about you and Uncle Jacy and Aunt Rita since I was this big." Emma held her hand out to her side. "She called Denny at the Marine base right away and told him, and I could practically hear him yelling all the way from Norfolk. Seeing you again has made Mom happier than I've seen her in a long time. Thanks."

"I really didn't do anything other than be at the right place at the right time — I guess," Skye said. "This whole thing has me going crazy, too. I've wanted to learn about my parents ever since I can remember, and now — "

"Would the camp folks mind if we'd sit here and chat a while?" Millie looked around the empty room.

"Oh, no," Skye said. "This is where the director said we should meet. Nobody will be in here again until five o'clock."

"That's great," Emma said. "Mom and I both work evening shifts, so we have lots of time to gab before we have to go."

Skye sat, and Millie and Emma joined her across the table. Skye wanted to start the conversation, but her exploding thoughts had her tongue all knotted up.

Emma immediately opened the album to the first page. "Mom and I thought you'd like to see what we all looked like over the last ten years. One thing we're not short on is family pictures."

"Skye," Millie said, "after your mom destroyed all your family photos, I realized how important it was to have roots, so I started taking pictures like crazy. I have four more albums like this. Oh, here's a copy of your picture that I promised." Millie pulled out the photo from her apron pocket.

"Thanks," Skye said. She studied the picture and then slipped it into her back jean pocket. "And I'm sure glad you took all these other pictures of your kids. Now I can get to know you much better."

"This is so exciting, I can hardly stand it," Emma said. "Denny said that he can't wait to meet you, but that won't be until his first leave at the end of the summer. Mom, how's that gonna work if Skye's in Pennsylvania?"

"We'll work something out, sweetie," Millie said.

"I'm sure Mom and Dad Chambers will do all they can to help us," Skye said. "They're really super."

"I can tell you really love them, Skye." Millie pulled the album in front of her. "And it's very obvious that they love you just as much."

"Did I tell you that Morgan's a foster child, too?" Skye asked.

"No, you didn't," Millie said, paging through the book as though she were looking for something. "What happened to her parents?" She stopped and looked at Skye.

"All Morgan knows is that her parents got divorced about four years ago and her dad went to California with another woman. Morgan's mom has a bunch of other kids and lives near Philly. She just couldn't handle Morgan's special needs, so she gave Morgan the choice to go to a 'facility' for kids like her or to go into foster care. Morgan's mom comes to see her only once or twice a year, which really tears Morgan up inside. Mom and Dad Chambers are really the only parents she's known for the last three years, and she thinks it was the best thing that ever happened to her."

"Hey, Skye!"

Skye turned and saw Morgan wheeling toward her from the kitchen.

"Hi, Morgan," Skye said. "You're not finished with work already, are you?"

Morgan eyed Millie and Emma as she approached the table. "Nah, I just took a five-minute break. I wanted to meet your cousin."

"It's nice to know you," Emma said. "I've already heard a lot about you from Mom."

"Skye and I have been best friends for a long time, so I'm interested in what's happening with her right now."

Hmm, she almost sounds too interested, Skye thought.

"Well, we're really glad that Mom met Skye at the diner," Emma said.

"And we're glad to know you, too," Millie said.

"Right," Morgan said, starting to wheel away. "Well, gotta get back to work. See you later, sis."

"Yeah, later," Skye said.

"She seems really nice," Millie said.

"Yeah," Skye said. "She's really cool." *But I'm wondering if she's missing her mom with all this going on with my family.*

"Mom, show Skye what you looked like when you were a kid. Those pictures are a riot."

"We can go through the book from cover to cover if Skye wants," Millie said.

"I'd really like to," Skye said. "We have a lot of time to catch up on."

"And we want you to tell us all about you, too," Emma said.

All afternoon Skye talked with her aunt and Emma. While Skye examined every last picture in the photo album, Millie and Emma filled her in on the Eister household and what had happened in their lives for the last eleven years. They talked about school and their jobs and how so very proud both of them were of Private Dennis Eister, U.S. Marine Corps. Millie also shared all the details about the day Skye was born and how cute she was as a toddler and how hard it was to give her up.

Then Skye had her turn to talk. As fast as her lips could move, she told them about all her foster homes, Keystone Stables, her horse Champ and her best friends—especially Chad. She also made a point to tell them about Jesus and how important he was in her life. When Skye glanced at her watch, she could hardly believe how the time had passed.

"Wow, it's already four o'clock," Skye said, standing. "I've got to get down to the barn and help cool down the horses. They should be back just about now from their long trail ride. I think Champ's the only one who got the day off."

Millie shuffled through the album, looking for something. "Wait a minute, Skye. I have something very important to show you." She pulled a small stack of envelopes from the back of the album. "Oh, here they are. I knew I had stuck those letters in here."

"What letters, Mom?" Emma asked.

"Skye," Millie said, "on Friday evening when I was driving home from the diner, it dawned on me that I might have something that'll help you track down your dad."

Skye's heart took off and her gaze darted from Millie's eyes to the letters in Millie's hands.

"These are all letters I wrote to your dad and Charlie Hamlock—the other inmate I knew." Millie flipped through the pile. Turning the last letter over, she handed it to Skye.

Skye saw that it had been addressed to her dad. "But why aren't any of these opened?"

"Remember I told you that your dad wouldn't see me or write? And remember I had said that I had written to Charlie for awhile, but he stopped writing?"

"Yep," Skye said.

"Well, these are all letters I had intended to mail, but I never did. I finally decided it was no use. Why I kept these letters all this time is beyond me."

"So how can they help Skye?" Emma asked as she examined a letter.

"Look on the back," Millie said. "It's not really the letters that will help. It's what's on the envelope."

"There's some kind of number here," Emma said. "Is that important?"

"You bet your booties," Millie said. "The average person can't just decide to send a letter to someone in the pen. The inmate will never get the letter unless that code number—it's called the 'inmate number'—is on the back. Without that, the prison returns the letter without the inmate ever seeing it."

Skye looked at the envelope and read, "LX-4102. So this was, or is, my dad's number."

"Yep, and here's Charlie's number, too." Millie handed Skye another envelope.

Skye read, "QH–9332."

"Hey, Mom, that's super," Emma said. "Skye can write and see if she gets a response—from either of them."

"I'm going to write, too, and see what happens," Millie said. "If either of them is there yet, they *just might* write back this time."

"Are the numbers ever changed?" Skye asked.

"No," Millie said. "I remember Charlie telling me that early on. He joked that he was stuck with that number for life."

"Is there anything in the letters that might be important?" Emma asked. "Or are they private and you don't want us to read them?"

"It's okay if you read them, but there's nothing in any of them that will help Skye," Millie said. "Skye, keep one letter from your dad and one from Charlie."

"What if they're not at that prison anymore?" Emma asked.

"Well, the way I understand it, the prison will forward the mail to the person if they know where he is," Millie said. "They'd definitely know if he's in another pen or at a halfway house. After that, I'm not sure if they keep track. So, if the letters come back—"

"I'll be up against another stone wall," Skye said.

kye hurried to the barn, and after she checked on Champ and gave him a big hug, she found Mrs. Chambers in a stall grooming Pepsi.

"Mom," Skye said, rushing to her foster mother's side, "Look what Millie gave me."

Mrs. Chambers poked back her Stetson and wiped her brow. "What do you have there, honey?"

Skye waved the letters in front of Mrs. Chambers. "She gave me real old letters that have some kind of inmate code on them for my dad and Charlie. She said if I write to them, they might write back. That is, if they're still in prison."

Mrs. Chambers took the envelopes from Skye and examined both sides. "My, that seems like a very good lead, Skye," she said. "But what if they're not there anymore?"

"Millie said that if the prison knows where the released inmates live, it will forward the mail to their new address. I want to write to them the first chance I get. But I'm not sure what to say. Will you help me?"

"Sure, the first chance we get." Mrs. Chambers handed the letters back to Skye. "Right now we've got to bed down these horses, and by then it will be suppertime."

"Mom," Skye said, "can we pray about this? If God's in this, then it will happen, don't you think?"

"I agree," Mrs. Chambers said. "And now would be a perfect time to pray about the whole matter."

As soon as Skye had finished her responsibilities on Monday evening, she and Mrs. Chambers made a beeline to the family's cabin and attacked the laptop and printer. Mrs. Chambers helped set up at a small table and then decided to crash on her bunk and read a book. Skye prepared to type two letters that she had been "Skye writing" in her brain all day long, and she decided to send her dad one of her school pictures that Mrs. Chambers always carried in her wallet. With Mr. Chambers and Morgan at the barn polishing tack, Skye had some private time with Mrs. Chambers.

Before Skye started to type, she leaned back in the chair and faced Mrs. Chambers. "Mom, I need to know how you feel about all this. Are you okay with it?"

Mrs. Chambers smiled, and her eyes seemed to penetrate into the depths of Skye's soul and read her very thoughts. She reached toward Skye and patted her hand. "Honey, right up front we want you to know that your dad and I love you very much, as though you were our own daughter, and we only want the best for you. I know that you've always needed to know something about your parents so you could come to grips with your past. We have absolutely no problem with your finding your roots. In fact, we've been praying about this moment since we took you in."

Skye stared deep into her foster mother's eyes, finding complete honesty that she knew was always there. "I don't know where I'd be if it wasn't for you and Dad," Skye said. "I just don't want to hurt you."

Mrs. Chambers' eyes filled with tears as she gave Skye another warm smile. "Skye, I don't want you to even think that way. You will not hurt us. We're very glad that God has opened this door for you. Your dad and I have discussed this numerous times, and—well—the possibility of your finding your parents is one reason we've been dragging our feet concerning adopting you. By all means we want to do that, but if your parents are in the picture, you might feel differently."

"I'll never feel different," Skye said. "I want to stay with you guys forever."

"That's a decision that only you can make," Mrs. Chambers said. "Over the years, we've worked with a lot of kids who had different ideas about their parents. Let's take Morgan, for example. She really doesn't want to stay in touch with her mother—or father. And you know she's told us those rare visits with her mother just bring up all those feelings of being abandoned. Maybe when she's older, she'll try to renew her relationship with them, but for now she's satisfied just living with us."

"I'm not so sure about that lately," Skye said.

"What do you mean?"

"I think she's been acting kinda strange about this whole business with my parents. Maybe she's thinking more about her own mom and dad these days."

"I did detect a little distance in her lately. She knows she can call her mother anytime she wants. We've encouraged her to do that."

"Well, at least she knows where her mom is," Skye said. "That's a big plus."

"Yes, and I believe that does make a difference," Mrs. Chambers said.

"Well, I'd sure like to know where my real mother is," Skye said, turning back to the computer.

"And, Skye," Mrs. Chambers said, "about these letters you're going to write. Just let the Lord take charge. We'll trust in him and see what happens."

"Mom," Skye said, "can I read the letters to you and then you can tell me how they sound?"

"Sure," Mrs. Chambers said. "Let me know when they're done."

After thirty minutes of typing and retyping, Skye asked her foster mother to join her at the table.

"Let's see these wonderful masterpieces," Mrs. Chambers said, smiling. Skye let her sit in front of the computer to read:

Dear Jacy,

I am your daughter, Skye Nicholson. I am thirteen years old and in the seventh grade. I've always wanted to know where you and Mom are. Just lately, I was given this address.

I live with two nice foster parents, Tom and Eileen Chambers, at Keystone Stables in central PA, a special-needs ranch and foster home. I have one foster sister, Morgan Hendricks. But right now we are near Charleston, SC, volunteering our time at another special-needs ranch. We brought four horses with us, and we are teaching the campers how to ride. My horse is a sorrel Quarter Horse. His name is Champ, and he's the most beautiful animal in the whole wide world.

I really want to get to know you. Please write me using the address on the envelope. We'll be here for twelve more days.

Your daughter Skye

Dear Mr. Hamlock,

I am Skye Nicholson, Jacy Nicholson's daughter and the niece of Millie Eister. She had written you letters for a while about ten years ago.

I am thirteen years old and am in foster care. I've always wanted to know where my parents are. Just lately, I found out that my father might be in the Brentwood prison. I have written him a letter and hope that he will write me back.

If my father is not there, Millie said you might be the only person who can help me find him. I really want to get to know him. I'm also searching for my mother.

If you know anything about either of them, will you please write and tell me what you know? I would be very grateful.

Millie told me that she is going to write to you too. I hope you write back. She's a nice lady.

Yours truly,
Skye Nicholson

From the time Skye mailed those important letters, she started to get up fifteen minutes earlier so she had time to check the Chambers' mailbox at the office for a letter from her dad or Charlie Hamlock.

On Thursday, Skye held an envelope addressed to Jacy Nicholson with the words RETURN TO SENDER stamped on the front, and her heart dropped like a rock to the bottom of her feet.

"Another stone wall," Skye said to Morgan back at the cabin. Mr. and Mrs. Chambers had already left for breakfast. Morgan was sitting at the cabin window, just staring. She didn't answer Skye.

"Morgan, what's the matter? You've just not been yourself lately."

"I already told you," Morgan said. "It's the same old thing. I want us to be friends forever."

"There's more to it than that," Skye said. "C'mon, tell me what's bugging you."

Morgan sniffled, then she forced out a stingy smile. "If you find them, do you want to go and live with them?" Suddenly, Morgan's eyes released a flood of tears that ran freely down her fiery red face.

"What?" Skye said. "C'mon, spill the beans, Morgan. What's bugging you?"

Morgan took a few deep, choppy breaths. Again, she wiped her cheeks. In all the time she had known Morgan, Skye had never seen her so upset.

"M-maybe I'm just being selfish," Morgan gasped, "but I'm going bonkers worrying that you're going to leave. You and Mr. and Mrs. Chambers are my family now. I don't want anything to spoil that. If you leave, nothing will ever be the same again at Keystone Stables."

In disbelief, Skye stared while Morgan just sobbed and sobbed. Without warning, tears burned in Skye's eyes, too, and her face flushed as she tried to figure out what to say to her very best friend.

"Morgan—"

"Oh, this is so stupid," Morgan cried. "I'm sorry, but I had to get this out. It's been bottled up inside me ever since we met Millie."

"No—no, that's okay." Skye took a deep breath. "Best friends tell all, and we're best friends. I want to know how you feel."

Morgan released a long, slow sigh. "Oh, Skye, I'm just afraid of losing my—my best friend."

"Morgan, you're never going to lose me as your best friend, no matter where I am."

"What does that mean?" Morgan's eyebrows peaked.

"It doesn't mean anything," Skye said. "I just want to find out where my parents are, that's all. As long as I can remember, I've always wanted to know my roots. To tell you the truth, I have no idea how I'm going to feel if I find them."

Morgan wiped her eyes and gave Skye her signature smile. "Just so we stay best buds, okay?"

"No problem." Skye gave Morgan a sincere smile. "I'll always think of you as my sister, too."

"I feel a whole lot better," Morgan said. "A *whole* lot better."

"Me too," Skye said. "Now let's get going. The horses and potatoes aren't going to wait all day for us."

With no response from her dad, Skye hoped and prayed all week that she'd hear something from the other inmate. "C'mon, Charlie. You gotta come through for me," she said before going for the mail every morning.

And Charlie did!

On Friday, Skye pulled a letter from the mailbox with her name and her present address scribbled on the envelope. With no return address anywhere, she tore it open and read a short note that appeared to have been written in a hurry:

Dear Skye, Your father is not here anymore. He was released early because he kept his nose clean. He left here about two years ago. He wrote to me for a while. The last I heard from him, he was living in Gatlinburg, Tennessee. Good luck trying to find him.

Charles P. Hamlock

In record time, Skye dashed back to the Chambers' cabin where she knew everyone was probably still sound asleep. She came to a skid stop at the door and glanced at her watch. *Almost six. It's time for them to get up anyway.* She burst through the doorway with absolutely no thought of restraining her excitement.

"Mom, Dad, I got a letter from Charlie!" She rushed to a bottom bunk and shook Mrs. Chambers' shoulder. "Mom, wake up. I've got the best news ever!" She pulled on her foster dad's arm that was dangling over the top bunk, then rushed to Morgan's bunk where she poked at Morgan. "Wake up, everybody. I have news about my dad!"

Morgan struggled to open her eyes, her frizzy red hair suffering from what looked like an all-night wrestling match with the pillow. Her wandering eyes finally focused on Skye as she yawned. "What has you going bonkers at this hour of the morning?"

"I heard from Charlie Hamlock," Skye bubbled, rushing back to the other set of bunks. By now, both Mr.

and Mrs. Chambers were leaning on their elbows, trying to get their wits about them.

"What's that, honey?" Mrs. Chambers asked. "What about Charlie?"

Mr. Chambers scratched his disheveled brown hair and yawned. "Well, you're certainly the loudest alarm clock I've ever heard."

"Dad, didn't you hear me?" Skye shoved the letter under his nose. "I heard from Charlie Hamlock. He said my dad might be living around Gatlinburg, Tennessee!"

"That's our girl," Mrs. Chambers chuckled. "Calm, cool, and collected."

Morgan sat up and looked in Skye's direction. "The last time I saw you this wound up, you and Champ had just won State in the Western Pleasure Class. Or was it when Chad winked at you last year at the Youth for Truth Christmas party? Cool it, girl." Morgan's usual friendly tone had an air of sarcasm.

She almost sounds angry, Skye thought. *What gives?* "This letter is better than any of that. I might be able to contact my dad."

Mr. Chambers took the letter in one hand and rubbed his eyes with the other. "Skye, we know you're terribly excited about this. We're just having a little fun with you. Now let me see what this says."

Skye's foster mother wiggled her way out of the bottom bunk. "Let me see this very important note."

Mr. Chambers handed her the letter, yawned again, and drew his fingers down over his mustache. "This *is* good news, Skye. Now we've got something to go on."

"When can we go to Gatlinburg, Dad? When?" Skye raked her fingers through her hair and chewed her lip.

"Hold your horses, honey." Mrs. Chambers handed the letter back to Skye. "This calls for a family powwow that will take more time than we have now. We've got to be at breakfast in a half hour and we have a full day of activities ahead for all of us."

"When can we talk about what to do next?" Skye's anxiety level had her mind churning like a windmill in a tornado.

Mr. Chambers threw off his sheet, swiveled on the mattress, and dropped to the floor next to his wife. His western pullover top and shorts matched Mrs. Chambers' outfit to a T. "Eileen, don't we have a free hour after supper tonight?"

Mrs. Chambers rubbed her eyes and thought for a moment. "Why, yes we do. The hayride doesn't start until around seven." Her glance darted from her husband to Skye. "After supper, we can all meet here and discuss this latest development."

Skye shifted to Morgan who had managed to position herself against the wall so she could watch the show. "Morgan, what are you doing after supper?"

"I'll be up to my ears in dirty pots and pans. I don't need to be in this meeting. You can fill me in later."

"Oh, that's right," Skye said. "I keep forgetting that somebody has to clean up the mess in the cafeteria every time we eat. I guess that's why they call it a 'mess hall.'"

"And camp critters sure can make messes," Mr. Chambers said with a sly grin. "Now, about our family meeting. Right after supper, we'll have our powwow here and see what we can do about Gatlinburg. Right now I could use a shower and a shave." He rubbed his stubby beard and smiled.

"Skye," Mrs. Chambers suggested, "if you have any time at all today, go online to that website we searched the other day. Now you can plug in 'Gatlinburg,' and it should tell you how many of those Jacy Nicholsons live in that area, if any."

"I hardly have time to breathe today," Skye said. "I have a full day of riding lessons right until supper."

"Well, the laptop will be waiting for you when you get back here then." Mrs. Chambers slipped her arm around Skye's shoulders.

"And let's keep this whole situation a matter of prayer all day long," Mr. Chambers said. "If God's in this, and I believe he is, then we'll find the right Mr. Jacy Nicholson."

Skye looked deep into her foster parents' eyes and beamed a broad smile. Then she glanced at Morgan, who had a strange, faraway look. *What is wrong with that girl? I thought everything was okay.*

All day Friday Skye and Champ worked their tails off in the squelching heat of the South Carolina sun. Although Skye enjoyed every minute with her horse and the camp kids, no matter how hot it was, her thoughts constantly drifted about 350 miles northwest to Gatlinburg, Tennessee, where she hoped and prayed she'd be able to find her real dad.

At suppertime, she gobbled down her hot dog and fries and made a mad dash to the family chalet. As she set up the laptop at the small table and went online, Mr. and Mrs. Chambers came in and joined her. As the three sat gawking at the screen, Skye typed in her real dad's name in the family and friends search engine. Three Jacy Nicholsons popped up for the Gatlinburg area along with their addresses, but only one had a phone number listed.

"Wow," Skye said, "there are three in or near that town. But only one has a phone number. Why don't the others list their phone numbers?"

"Skye," Mr. Chambers said, "the Internet has become very intrusive in people's personal lives. It's enough that the site posts people's addresses. Some folks would rather not even have that out there as common knowledge. My guess is that they want their phone numbers unlisted."

"Or maybe they have cell phones and don't want that number shared," Skye reasoned.

"What surprises me is that there are three men in that same area with such an unusual name," Mrs. Chambers said. "That's amazing."

"Are there any websites where we could find more information about any of them?" Skye wrote down the one phone number and then sat poised, her fingers ready to type.

"Well," Mr. Chambers said, "why don't you plug 'Jacy Nicholson' in a few search engines and see what happens. The men might have businesses or sell products that they're advertising on their own websites."

"Good idea, Dad," Skye said as she started to type.

In seconds, the screen displayed "No Match."

"Well," Skye said, "Besides three addresses, I have this one phone number. Could I call this guy right now? He just might be my father."

"Skye," Mrs. Chambers said, "have you thought at all about what you plan to say? You can't call and just blurt out, 'Hello, this is your long-lost daughter. Can we talk?'"

Skye pursed her lips and folded her arms. "I see what you mean. That would definitely be a total shock."

"Why don't you think about it awhile," Mr. Chambers said. "The first words you say will be very important. And if he has voice mail, would you want to leave a message? That's something else that's very important to think about."

Skye slumped back in her chair and sighed. "You're right, Dad. Can I try calling in an hour?"

"Whenever you feel that you're ready," Mr. Chambers said gently.

"I probably shouldn't leave a message," Skye said. "If it would be the wrong Jacy, he wouldn't know what in the world I'm talking about. And even if it would be the right one, I'd rather talk to him directly."

"A wise decision," Mr. Chambers said.

Mrs. Chambers swiveled her chair to the side of the table and faced her husband. "Tom, you don't have anything pressing back home next week, do you?"

Mr. Chambers sat, still staring at the screen. With his chin resting on clenched fists, his thoughts were far away.

"Dad?" Skye poked the man's shoulder.

"Huh? Oh, sorry. Just thinking," Mr. Chambers finally said. "I didn't schedule any appointments for my computer business for the whole week after this trek. It takes me that long to get back into the groove of 'life' again after any trip, no matter where we go. So, if you're asking if we can go to Gatlinburg next week, the answer is yes."

"Do you really mean it?" Skye's voice reached its highest octave. "We can actually try to find my father?"

Mrs. Chambers gave Skye a warm smile. "Honey, we can do this. We have the time."

"And I think we might be able to mix some business with pleasure, if you know what I mean," Mr. Chambers said.

"Tom, are you thinking what I'm thinking?" Mrs. Chambers asked.

Mr. Chambers gave his wife one of his sly grins. "Skye, plug in 'AQHA' and see if the American Quarter Horse Association is sponsoring any horse shows in the Gatlinburg area."

"Horse shows?" Skye asked and paused. "Oh, I get it," she said, starting to type.

Mr. Chambers relaxed in his chair and folded his arms. "If there are any horse shows in that part of Tennessee—and I'm sure there are this time of the year—we can register ASAP and compete. When we get to Gatlinburg, we can't be looking for Jacy Nicholson twenty-four/seven, so if we enter a horse show or two, we might win some prize money to help us with our expenses. And I'm sure our four equines don't want to face a week of nothing but munching hay and snoozing."

"Tom, that's an excellent idea," Mrs. Chambers said. "We can check out the KOA campgrounds with accommodations for large pets. Some of those campsites have makeshift barns for fur-friends like ours. When we find a suitable camp, we'll drive down our stakes there for as long as necessary." She glanced at Skye, who was engrossed with the information on the screen. "And although it looks like our gal isn't into the tourist mode at the moment, Gatlinburg and Pigeon Forge have some very nice attractions that we might be able to check out."

"We'd have to call Chad and ask if he'll stay at Keystone Stables a few more days. Wait until he hears about my father." Skye was totally oblivious to Mrs. Chambers' last words. "Look here. There are two western AQHA shows right in the Gatlinburg area next week."

"Then it's settled," Mr. Chambers said. "Come Sunday after church, we're on our way to Tennessee."

Skye held up the piece of paper with the phone number. "And if this isn't my father, the first thing I'm going to do is find a new phone book and see if the other Jacys might be listed," Skye said. "The locator website just might be outdated."

chapter eight

A n hour later, and every hour thereafter until bed-time, Skye called the number for Jacy Nicholson Number One. When no one answered, she went to bed disappointed.

All day Saturday while she taught riding lessons and helped with a hayride, she called the number every hour on the hour with the same result.

Sunday after church, the Chambers' family said their teary farewells at the ranch and set their sights on Gatlinburg. Again, all afternoon and into the night, Skye had no success with the phone. "This guy has got to be on a vacation or something," she groaned in the truck cab and flipped the cell phone shut after her last try around 9 p.m. For a while, Skye's mouth ran nonstop about trying to find her father, but soon pure exhaustion wooed her into a sound sleep. Her dreams flitted from her father to horse shows to the kids she had just left behind to Chad and then back to her missing dad again ... *Jacy Nicholson ... What if he doesn't want to see me ... Does he have other kids now? ... Which Jacy is it? ... Maybe it's none of them ...*

Close to midnight, the Chambers family pulled into a KOA campground on the outskirts of Pigeon Forge. After Mr. Chambers registered at the office, he, Mrs. Chambers, and Skye bedded down the horses in a small pole barn, then they and Morgan crashed in the bunks in the log cabin and were asleep in seconds.

At seven o'clock the next morning while Mr. and Mrs. Chambers prepared breakfast at a small brick fireplace and camper's table in front of the cabin, Skye hurried to the camp office with one goal in mind: to find a phone book.

"Mom! Dad!" Skye yelled as she charged back to camp. Mr. Chambers was stirring his trademark scrambled eggs in a pan on the fire while Mrs. Chambers buttered biscuits at the table. The table hosted a mishmash of paper plates and cups, plastic utensils, and a quart container of orange juice. Morgan sat by the fire holding a marshmallow on a stick over the low flame.

"Sounds like you have some good news." Morgan's glance darted from the marshmallow to Skye then back.

"There are two Jacy Nicholsons in the phone book," Skye said. "One number is the same as what I found online. Can I call them both now? Can I?"

"Skye, I hate to keep saying this," Mrs. Chambers said, smiling, "but you'll have to hold your horses again." She glanced at her watch and went back to her buttering job. "It's not even 7:15 yet."

Mr. Chambers lifted the frying pan and shifted to the table where he scraped the eggs into a large plastic serving dish. He then set the pan on the ground beside the fireplace. "Skye, we have to think this through. If those guys are up and about at this hour on a Monday morning, they're probably getting ready for work or whatever."

Skye flopped on a canvas chair near the table. "If, and that's a big if, Jacy Nicholson Number One is even around here. Maybe he moved."

Mrs. Chambers poured four glasses of orange juice. "Skye, I'm sure that sooner or later you're going to get through to one of these men."

"At this hour of the day, they'd probably think it's a prank call and slam the phone down quicker than you could say, 'Dada,'" Morgan said. She wheeled her Jazzy to the one side of the table, plopped her gooey burnt mess onto a paper plate, and giggled. "Scrambled eggs and marshmallows. What a treat."

"Only a teenager would come up with such a gross combination," Mr. Chambers kidded.

"Skye, honey," Mrs. Chambers said, "You need to put yourself in those men's shoes. Even if one of them is your dad, you should try to be careful what you say and how you say it."

Skye's mind churned out her next plan while she gazed at two local phone numbers scribbled on a small piece of paper. "I've been thinking a lot about that," she said. "I'll try to let him know kind of slow and easy that he's talking to his daughter."

"It's going to be quite a shock, no matter how careful you are," Mrs. Chambers said.

Mr. and Mrs. Chambers settled at the table and Mr. Chambers prayed. Then the four dug into their campfire breakfast. "I would suggest waiting until around ten o'clock or so before you call," Mr. Chambers said. "If either of those men is your father, we can make plans to meet him as soon as he's able to do so."

"That's *if* either of them answers the phone," Morgan said. "They're probably working. Of course, they could be on later shifts, too. That's a possibility."

"Skye, you do have one big plus in your favor." Mrs. Chambers placed a scoopful of eggs on her plate then took a bite. "Your aunt said that your dad loved you dearly. It's my guess that he is longing to see you, and he'll be ecstatic when you find him."

Mr. Chambers scooped some eggs and held the spoon in front of Morgan. "Ready for the best eggs in the world?"

"Yep," she said, "dump them right on top of my marshmallow, please."

"On top of that?" he said in mock disbelief. "Girl, you must have a cast iron stomach."

"Oh, Tom, just give the girl her eggs." Mrs. Chambers chuckled. "If Morgan's going to be a chef, she'll want to try different foods."

"Yeah," Morgan said. "Someday I'll have a restaurant and feature entrees for 'The Foolish and the Brave.'"

"You've got a good start right here," Mr. Chambers said.

Skye had tuned herself in and out of the present conversation while she planned what to say on the phone. Finally, she said, "I think I know exactly what I'm going to say and how I'm going to say it."

"Let's hear it, and we'll all take a vote," Morgan said.

"Dad," Skye said, "will you pretend to be the voice on the other end of the phone? Let's practice."

"Sure." Mr. Chambers chuckled with a mouthful of eggs. "Wait until I get the egg off my face."

The next few hours dragged on like a turtle strolling through molasses. After Skye helped clean up the breakfast mess, she went to the pole barn and fed the horses, mucked the stalls, and cleaned their hooves. She also gave each horse a quick once-over with currycomb and brush, but when she got to Champ, she pampered him like a mare with a newborn foal. As usual, she spilled her guts to him while he chomped on his grain and listened with twitching ears and a series of nickers.

"Champ," she said, combing the horse's mane, "I just don't know what I'm going to do if I find my real dad. What if he doesn't want to see me?"

Champ nickered and nibbled at his bucket of oats.

"And I don't want to hurt Mom and Dad Chambers. Ever. They're just being so super about all of this. But what about Morgan? Something's been bugging her, and I've got to find out what. She's just—just different lately. I think what I need to do is pray more about this whole Jacy business. What do you think?"

Nicker, nicker.

"You're right. Now would be a good time." Skye laid the grooming tools on the ground, leaned her arms on Champ's back, and folded her hands. "Dear Jesus," she prayed, "first of all, I'd like to ask you to forgive me for lousing up, which I seem to do a lot sometimes. Next, I need your help to find my parents. Please help me to know what to say when I do find them. Lord, I ask that you help me to be brave and love them no matter what happens. And if they don't know about you, please help me to tell them what you've done in my life. Now about Morgan, I ask that you help her with whatever's bothering her, and help me to understand what she's going through. Thanks for such great foster parents and thanks for everything else you've given me at Keystone Stables, especially Champ. Oh, and please bless Chad, too. In Jesus' name I pray. Amen."

Nicker, nicker.

At ten o'clock sharp, Skye sat on her bunk and tried to call both Jacy Nicholsons. Her foster parents and Morgan encircled Skye, giving her moral support. Again, the one number rang and rang–and rang—with no answer; the other number clicked on a voice mail recording, so Skye shut off the cell phone without leaving any message. "Now what?" she grumbled.

"Skye," Mrs. Chambers said, "I know you don't want to hear about being patient again, but we have no choice. It seems like the one man might be away. The other one might be working. I suggest you call around noon. If there's still no answer, you can try every few hours."

"Couldn't we just go and find their homes?" Skye rattled off. "We have their addresses. Then there's the third man who doesn't have a phone number. We don't have any way of contacting him except by going to his house. His address is 690 Sassafras Street."

"I think it's best if you try to contact the two by phone first," Mr. Chambers said. "If one of them is your dad, he'll need some time to grasp hold of the whole situation."

Morgan flipped her long red hair back. "Yeah, he might feel like fainting or dropping his teeth or something, and he wouldn't want to do that in front of perfect strangers."

"I'll tell you what we can do." Mrs. Chambers' eyes sparkled with excitement. "Let's go into Pigeon Forge for a few hours. We can't sit around here twiddling our thumbs. There are plenty of tourist attractions to keep us busy. Skye, you can try those numbers again at noon no matter where we are."

Mr. Chambers smoothed his mustache and squared his tan Stetson. "And later today we need to pretty the horses and polish the tack for the horse show tomorrow. We need to be there at 9 a.m. sharp for Skye's first entry."

"I hope I can concentrate," Skye said. "No need to worry, though. Champ knows the Western Pleasure routine like he invented it. I'm sure he'll pull me through."

"Skye," Mrs. Chamber said, "don't put yourself under any undue pressure. The horse show is just a little something extra for all of us to enjoy while we're here."

"That's right." Mr. Chambers poked back his hat. "Winning is all fine and dandy, but it's not the most important thing. Just have a good time."

Within a half hour, the Chambers family loaded up in their truck and headed into Pigeon Forge. All day and into early evening they enjoyed the area's most popular attraction, the Dollywood theme park. Although Skye loved theme parks, her mind was constantly on who and where her real dad was. At twelve o'clock, four, and six,

Skye called the phone numbers with no response. Finally, on the family's way back to the campground at eight o'clock, Skye called the first number and got a response:

"Hello, Jacy Nicholson speaking."

Skye froze.

"Hello?" the man repeated. "Nicholson residence."

"Ah—Mr. Nicholson?"

"Yes."

"My name is Skye Nicholson. My birthday is on January 15ᵗʰ and I'm thirteen years old. I'm a foster child from central Pennsylvania, and I'm looking for my real father, Jacy Nicholson. Would that be you?"

After a short pause, Skye heard, "I'm sorry, young lady. That wouldn't be me. I'm sixty-five years old. I'm married and my wife and I have three grown sons, but no missing daughter. I hope you find your dad. Good-bye now."

"Wait!" Skye said. "Would you happen to know who the other Jacy Nicholson is in the phone book?" She read him the number.

"Why, yes," Mr. Nicholson said. "That's my son. He's in his forties. He's married but he has two sons. He's never had a daughter either."

Skye took a deep breath before asking her next question. "Sir, do you know the other Jacy Nicholson who lives in this area?"

"Hmm," Mr. Nicholson said. "I wasn't even aware that another man by that name lives around here. My son and I are the only ones listed in the phone book. Are you sure there's a third Jacy in this area? That's incredible."

"Yep, I found his name and address on the Internet," Skye said.

"Well, young lady," Mr. Nicholson said, "I wish you the best in finding your father. I'm sorry I couldn't be more help. Good luck."

Skye's eyes burned like fire as they flooded with tears. "Th-thank you, Mr. Nicholson," she said, yearning in the depths of her soul that she were talking with her dad. "Goodbye." Skye flipped the phone shut and slumped back in the seat of the truck like she had lost her best friend.

"That didn't sound too good," Mrs. Chambers said from the front of the cab.

"He's not my dad," Skye groaned. "And the other man is his son, and he never had a daughter either."

"Well," Mr. Chambers said. "The first thing we'll do tomorrow after the horse show is go find Mr. Jacy Nicholson Number Three."

Skye nudged Morgan with her elbow. "Tomorrow's another day, Sis, and I just might hit the jackpot."

"Just might," Morgan said without looking in Skye's direction.

chapter nine

Skye chewed her lip as she sat on Champ outside the AQHA show ring. She had her hair drawn back into a bun, adorned by a dark brown suede cowboy hat complete with hawk feather and leather braid, leveled on her head to her eyebrows. She wore a red-checkered shirt and a leather-fringed vest with the number "8" pinned on the back, a blue necktie, cowhide gloves, chaps, and brown leather-cut boots. Skye looked like the perfect match for her mount. Champ had on his polished bridle with blue brow band and a leather-cut saddle that highlighted his glistening coat and silky mane and tail. Both sparkled in the already sizzling Tennessee morning sun, and although Skye's thoughts drifted constantly to Jacy Nicholson Number Three, she was raring to show her pride and joy.

In the southern humidity and heat, the smell of sweating horses and manure permeated the hazy air. Skye wiped a bead of sweat from her brow and scanned the horse trailers parked outside of the ring. Her glance shifted to the bleachers with a few avid horse fans, the announcer's stand blaring incessant noise, and the handful of judges busy comparing notes on their clipboards. At the long end of the large oval corral, Skye rode Champ to join five other entries in her class. They were huddled on the outside of the gate, tightening cinch straps, adjusting stirrups, checking bits in their horses' mouths, and sliding their hat strings tighter to their chins. Her gaze drifted back to the other end of the corral where Mr. and Mrs. Chambers stood with Morgan on her mount, Blaze. All were watching with great interest.

As Skye waited to enter the ring, her mind wandered again to the first time she had ever ridden Champ in a horse show, just a few months after she had moved into Keystone Stables. Her life had changed so much since then! God had transformed her from a wild juvenile delinquent foster kid to a Christian young lady with purpose in life. He had saved her from a life of sin and heartache and had placed her in the best foster home any kid could ever hope to have. "And to top it all off, I have the most beautiful horse in the whole world," she said, reaching down and petting Champ's smooth sorrel neck.

"Attention, ladies and gentlemen," the loud speaker echoed, "the Intermediate Western Pleasure Class is now entering the gate."

The gate swung outward, and horses and riders entered the ring, walking single-file along the perimeter of the fence.

Skye took a deep breath, squared her hat, and squeezed Champ with her legs. She straightened her back and smiled, focusing on her horse's moves as he brought up the end of the line and entered the ring.

For the next few minutes, Skye and Champ put on an outstanding performance, one that won them a second place red ribbon and enough prize money to pay for their KOA cabin rental. Skye was ecstatic, giving most of the credit where credit was due. "Champ outdid himself," she told Mr. and Mrs. Chambers. "He is some horse."

By three o'clock that same day, the Chambers' clan was loading four horses, five ribbons, and $375 prize money into their transport. Despite the excitement of the day, Skye's thoughts were never far from her missing dad.

"Skye, I'll tell you what we can do now," Mr. Chambers said as he scooped up Morgan from her wheelchair and placed her in the truck cab. "We'll take the horses back to the campground, make a quick clothes change, then go on a Jacy hunt."

By four o'clock, the Chambers family was hot on the trail of Jacy Nicholson Number Three, Gatlinburg, Tennessee. After a stop for directions at a mini-mart, Mr. Chambers parked the truck in front of 690 Sassafras Street, a beige stucco bungalow with a small manicured yard on the outskirts of town.

Skye and Mrs. Chambers walked to the front door, and Skye, with a trembling hand, rang the doorbell.

A long minute later, the door opened.

"Yes?" a woman said with an apprehensive smile.

The woman in her mid-thirties, Skye guessed, had a short, slim frame. Her kinky brown hair rested gently on her shoulders, and friendly hazel eyes accented a tan face with a hint of make-up. She wore a pink pullover sport shirt, navy blue capris, and brown sandals.

"Is Mr. Jacy Nicholson here?" Skye returned the apprehensive smile.

"Who should I say is asking?" the woman said.

"I'm Skye Nicholson," Skye said.

"And I'm her foster mother, Eileen Chambers," Mrs. Chambers said. "We live in central Pennsylvania."

"I'd—I'd like to ask Mr. Nicholson a question," Skye said.

The woman's pretty face portrayed an expression that Skye couldn't read.

Could she be my real mother? Skye pondered. *Maybe they got back together.*

"Hon," the woman yelled back inside. "There's someone here who wants to meet you."

Skye grabbed her foster mother's hand and said a quick prayer. *Dear God, please let this be him.*

In seconds, a lanky man in his mid-thirties with thinning dark brown hair combed straight back and brown eyes came to the door. He had on a gray T-shirt, faded blue jeans, and black sneakers. "What is it, Ruth?" he said, focusing on Skye and Mrs. Chambers.

Ruth? Not my mother, Skye thought.

"This young lady says her name is Skye Nicholson, and she's asking if you know her."

"Skye?" the man asked. "Skye Nicholson?"

Mr. Nicholson stared at Skye like she had just appeared out of thin air. His mouth hung open, but no words came out.

Ruth nudged the man while she focused on Skye. "Jacy, what's the matter? Say something."

Skye stared back at the man and found herself mirroring his reaction. Finally, she found her courage and spoke. "Mr. Nicholson," her voice quivered, "I—I'm a foster kid from central Pennsylvania, and I'm looking for my parents. This is my foster mother, Eileen Chambers."

"Hello." Mrs. Chambers nodded.

"Nice to know you," Ruth said.

Mr. Nicholson just stared.

Skye punched her thumb over her shoulder. "My foster dad and foster sister are out in the truck. I'm thirteen years old, and I was born on January 15th in Pittsburgh. I'm looking for my father. Are—are you my father?"

The man's face drained of all its color as his eyes grew red and moist. "Skye? You're ... my daughter, Skye?" he stammered.

Skye felt the air rush from her lungs in a single, unplanned gust. "It appears that maybe I am," she said, her lips trembling slightly as she tried to smile.

Ruth's face beamed with obvious delight, slipping her arm around Jacy's. "Oh, my, this is too wonderful for words. He's told me over and over that he's been searching for you for years." She nudged the man again. "Jacy, for heaven's sake, say something. You do want them to come in, don't you?"

"Oh, yes, of course." His stare riveted on Skye, Mr. Nicholson stepped back and swept his hand in a gesture of welcome. "Please come in. And tell the others to come in too."

Mrs. Chambers turned toward the truck and waved. "Come on in!" she yelled to Mr. Chambers and Morgan.

"And I'll get some snacks and sweet tea," Ruth said and hurried out of the foyer.

Skye stepped inside, never looking away from Jacy Nicholson Number Three—her father! *What should I do? Should I give him a hug? Shake his hand? What should I say?* Though she had rehearsed exactly what she wanted to say and do, Skye's emotions were exploding, forcing her to struggle to make sense of the wonderful, yet absolutely frightening, moment in which she found herself. With her entire body trembling, she took quick breaths to keep up with her racing heart. All she could do was stare with watery eyes.

Mr. Nicholson's eyes flooded with tears as he made an obvious attempt to sort out his emotions as well. His face betrayed mixed emotions—utter shock and pure delight, and Skye noticed his lips quiver, as though he was trying to speak. But he could do nothing but stare back. "Can—can I give you a hug?" he finally managed to say, his glance darting from Skye to Mrs. Chambers and back.

Skye froze on the spot, everything around her in a complete blur but her father's eyes. "Yes, sir," she said, staring, searching. *This man is my father! My real father!* she kept thinking over and over, convincing herself that it really was true.

Mr. Nicholson carefully wrapped his arms around Skye like she was made of paper. He squeezed gently, Skye did the same, and then they both backed away. A pleasant after-shave aroma filled Skye's nostrils and she smiled. *Canoe! That's the same stuff I bought Dad—um, Dad Chambers—for Christmas last year,* Skye thought.

Skye felt stranger than she had ever felt in her entire life. She desperately wanted to love, and be loved by Jacy Nicholson, whom she now could call her father. *But how?* she pondered. *How do I love someone I don't even know?*

"Skye," he sniffled, wiping streams of tears from his cheeks, "this is an answer to prayer. I've wondered all these years where you were. Please sit down and tell me all about yourself."

He led Skye and Mrs. Chambers into a small living room. With natural wood paneling, modest beige furniture, and a brown oval rug nestled on hardwood floors, the tiny den's coziness overpowered its confinement. Not a hint of dust or clutter made a statement anywhere.

Mr. Nicholson gestured toward a brown plaid sofa. "Please have a seat."

Skye and Mrs. Chambers sat on cushions that almost enfolded them in softness. Skye leaned forward, clenched her sweaty hands, and rested her arms on her knees.

Mr. Nicholson sat in a fluffy cream-colored recliner and mirrored Skye's posture. "Skye, I don't know where to begin. I've rehearsed this moment in my mind for years, planning exactly what I'd say to you when I finally found you, and now—well—since you found me, I'm speechless. I guess the best thing I can do is let you ask questions."

"Hello?" Mr. Chambers yelled in the opened front door.

"Come right in, folks," Mr. Nicholson said.

"Thank you!" Mr. Chambers came in carrying Morgan. He walked into the room and placed Morgan next to Skye.

"Mr. Nicholson," Mrs. Chambers said, "this is my husband, Tom, and our other foster daughter, Morgan Hendricks."

"Hi," Morgan said.

"Nice to meet you," Mr. Nicholson said.

"We're very pleased to meet you," Mr. Chambers said as the men shook hands.

"Please sit down," Mr. Nicholson offered.

"Thank you," Mr. Chambers said, sitting in a chair next to the sofa.

Mrs. Nicholson came in carrying a tray with pretzels and six glasses of iced tea. She placed them on an end table next to Mr. Nicholson's chair. "I'm sure you folks would love something cool," she said as she handed out the drinks.

"Thank you," they all said, taking the glasses.

"Ruth, slow down a minute so I can introduce you," Mr. Nicholson said. "Folks, this is my wife, Ruth."

Mr. Nicholson grabbed a glass and then passed the pretzels. "Help yourself," he said, smiling.

Skye never took her stare away from the man.

"Thanks." Mr. Chambers took the bowl, grabbed a pretzel and passed the bowl to his wife.

Mrs. Nicholson opened a folding chair, placing it next to her husband. She sat, sipped her tea, and gave a warm smile. Almost in unison, the Chambers family did the same.

"Now that we're all settled," Mr. Nicholson directed his attention toward his daughter, "go ahead. Ask all the questions you'd like."

As the others sipped tea, Skye chewed on her lip. Desperately, she tried to sort out dozens of questions that had her brain tied up in one big knot, searching for the one question that meant more to her than anything else in the world. Finally, as though one determined question crowded its way to the front of a busy line, Skye took a quick breath. "Where's my mother?"

chapter ten

G od forgive me," Mr. Nicholson lamented. "I was hoping and praying that you could tell me where Rita is. What I put that woman through—"

Ruth gently grasped her husband's hand. "Hon, that was a long time ago and a part of your other life."

"Other life?" Mr. Chambers asked.

Mr. Nicholson patted his wife's hand, relaxed into his recliner and took a deep breath. "Before I say anything else, I'd like to know how you folks found me."

"The Internet," Mrs. Chambers said.

"Well, partly," Skye said. "By accident, we met Millie last week. I never even knew your name, or my real mother's name, or that I had an aunt. We went into a restaurant, and this waitress, Millie, overheard my name, asked who I was, and said she's my aunt. She works at the Cozy Cupboard near Charleston."

Mr. Nicholson leaned forward as his eyebrows peaked. "You met Millie?"

"Jacy's been looking for her for years," Ruth said. "I hope you have her address."

"Oh, we do," Mrs. Chambers said. "And her phone number."

Ruth hurried toward the kitchen. "I'll get paper and a pen so we can write that down."

"And I'll call her today," Jacy added. "No wonder I couldn't find her. I still had her Pennsylvania address and phone number."

"Do you know—oh, I guess you don't—that Denny's in the Marines, and Emma's going to college next year?" Skye asked.

"That's wonderful," Mr. Nicholson said. "I can't believe those kids are that old. Time sure flies by. What were you folks doing in Charleston?"

"We volunteered at a special-needs ranch with our four horses," Mrs. Chambers said. "It was only God's perfect timing that we met Millie. She told us all she knew about you."

"Then you know I've been in prison." Mr. Nicholson's face morphed into a look of shame.

"Yes," Skye said, "but that doesn't matter to any of us. Before I went to live with Mom and Dad Chambers, I had a record as long as a flag pole and was headed for lockup."

"But that was *your* other life." Mr. Chambers gave Skye a warm smile then addressed Mr. Nicholson. "We're Christians, and when Skye accepted Christ, he changed her life completely."

Morgan's freckled face beamed a smile. "And Jesus has helped me deal with my cerebral palsy. Because of him, I learned to cope." She worked on a pretzel and sipped her tea.

Skye smiled at Morgan and thought, *I'm glad she finally said something. It's not like her to be so quiet.*

Mr. Nicholson asked Morgan, "Young lady, how long have you been a member of the Chambers clan?"

"For three years, sir," Morgan said. "And I've loved every minute of it."

Mrs. Nicholson came back and handed a pen and pad to Mr. Chambers.

"One moment," Mr. Chambers said. He sandwiched his glass between his boots and took the paper and pen from Mrs. Nicholson. He pulled out his wallet from his back pocket, filtered through a pack of cards and pulled out a folded paper. "I can't really tell you when to try to contact Millie," he said while he copied Millie's information. "She works all kinds of crazy shifts." He handed the paper to Mr. Nicholson.

"We'll keep trying until we do," Mr. Nicholson said, studying the paper. "Ruth, wait until you hear this. These folks are Christians."

"Well, praise the Lord," Mrs. Nicholson said as she sat down.

"We're Christians, too," Mr. Nicholson said. "I came to know Christ as my Savior in prison, and it's best thing that ever happened to me. Ruth worked with a prison evangelism ministry, and I met the Lord through her. I got out of the pen two years ago, and then we got married at a little chapel in Gatlinburg. We liked it so much here we decided to stay. I'm an auto mechanic at a big car dealership here in town, and Ruth is a beautician at the Smoky Mountain Mall. I can't begin to tell you how good God's been to me after all the rotten things I've done." The man wiped his eyes and released a heart-felt smile.

"Mr. Nicholson, God's in the business of saving *rotten* folks like us," Mrs. Chambers said. "We've all done things we're not proud of. Thank God, we know Jesus as our Savior, and those things are forgiven and forgotten."

"That sure is the truth," Mr. Nicholson said. "And folks, please call us Jacy and Ruth."

"All right," Mrs. Chambers said, "but only if you'll call us by our first names, too."

"It's a deal, Eileen," Ruth said, then took a sip of tea.

"And Skye," Jacy said, "you'll have to decide what you want to call me. It's up to you."

"I'll definitely give it some serious thought," Skye said, smiling.

"Now, Morgan," Jacy said, "you were about to tell me how you got hooked up with these folks."

"I really don't want to hog Skye's time with you—"

"Don't worry about that." Mrs. Chambers gave the girls a sly smile. "When Skye's mouth starts moving, it won't stop until midnight."

Everyone chuckled.

"Oh, Mom," Skye said, giggling.

"Go ahead," Mr. Chambers said to Morgan. "Fill the man in."

"Well," Morgan pushed her hair behind her shoulders, "there's really not much to tell. About five years ago, my father took off and headed to California with another woman. Mom had three other kids besides me. Since she's never been a very stable person, she couldn't cope with all my special needs. She had to put me into foster care, and I got bounced around for two years until I came to live with Mr. and Mrs. C."

"Do you ever see your parents?" Ruth asked.

"Nah." A look of regret swept over Morgan's face. "I don't even know where Dad is now. Mom lives near my Aunt Martha somewhere in Philly, but Mom's so busy with three kids and working, she hardly ever calls. Last Christmas I saw her for a few hours, but we just don't keep in touch. I consider Mr. and Mrs. C. and Skye my real family. I love them a whole bunch."

"And we love you, Morgan," Mrs. Chambers said.

"She's just like a real sister!" Skye gave Morgan a thumbs-up.

"I want to know so much about all of you, but I don't know where to start," Jacy said.

"We feel the same way," Mr. Chambers said. "But at least God has brought us together, and we can start at the beginning."

"How long are you folks going to be in this area, and where are you heading next?" Ruth asked.

"We came specifically to find you," Mrs. Chambers said. "I guess we'll stay a day or two yet; after that we'll head back to Pennsylvania."

Jacy took a bite of pretzel. "How is the good old Keystone State? Ruth and I miss some parts of it, but not the nasty winters."

"The good old Keystone State is doing fine," Mr. Chambers said, glancing at his wife. "And lately, we've been having mild winters. I'd say we've probably averaged only about twenty inches of snow each of the last few years."

"That's right." Mrs. Chambers nodded. "And the frigid temps have been staying north of us. Our last few winters really haven't been that bad."

"Jacy, did you know there are two other Jacy Nicholsons in this area?" Morgan asked.

"Yeah," Jacy said. "I've seen their names in the phone book. I guess I should have my name listed, too, but when I first got out of prison, I was a little skittish. You know, I really should get my name in there. There's no need to be unlisted."

"We're in our church directory," Ruth said, "and almost all of our friends are from church, so we didn't really see the need—until now."

"Skye, there are so many questions I have to ask you," Jacy said. "Can you folks stay for supper?"

"Can we, Dad?" Skye asked Mr. Chambers, and then her face turned beet red as her glance darted from Mr. Chambers to Jacy. "Oh, sorry. I guess I'll have to make it clear which dad I'm talking to. I've really got to think this through."

Jacy chuckled and gave his daughter a warm smile. "It'll take some time, Skye. There's no rush. So folks, how about staying for supper?"

"Oh, please do," Ruth said. "We have some cold cuts and I'll whip up a quick salad. It won't be anything fancy, but we'd love to have you."

"We'd be glad to stay," Mr. Chambers said.

Ruth glanced at her watch and stood. "There's no time like the present to get it moving. I can have the food ready in a jiffy. Hon, should we eat at the picnic table in the backyard?"

"What's your pleasure, folks?" Jacy asked.

"We love picnics!" Skye said.

"Then a picnic it'll be," Ruth said, turning toward the kitchen.

Mrs. Chambers stood. "Ruth, I'd love to help you. That way we can get to know each other."

"Sure." Ruth gestured for Mrs. Chambers to follow. "I'd love the company."

"Let me know if you need any more help," Jacy yelled after his wife.

"There's not much to do with cold cuts," she yelled back. "We gals can manage. You just enjoy getting to know your daughter."

As Mrs. Chambers left the room, Jacy focused on Skye and shook his head. "I still can't believe this is true. Skye, just start from scratch and tell me all about yourself. Maybe with your Aunt Millie's help, we can track down your mother. Rita was scared to death of me when they sent me up. She divorced me, changed her name, and went into hiding. But that's all I know. I need to find that woman and tell her I'm not the man I used to be. I have no hard feelings against her at all. I'm just so sorry about everything that has happened. I need to apologize to her for all the pain I've caused her."

"With God on our side I think we will find her some-how," Skye said. "I just hope she's still alive."

"Why'd you say that?" Jacy asked. "Did Millie say Rita was sick or something?"

"No, Aunt Millie doesn't know anything about her," Skye said. "But all my life I've wanted to get to know my real mother. I just hope she doesn't die before I find her."

"I don't even know where to begin," Jacy said, "but I've got to help find her and make things right."

t 7 a.m. Thursday morning, after a tearful farewell and promises to keep in touch with the Nicholsons, the Chambers family and their four horses headed toward Pennsylvania. In about eleven hours, they pulled into Keystone Stables, and an eager welcoming committee greeted the travelers home.

Chad, with his dimpled smile, and the two Westies, Tippy and Ty, waited anxiously in front of the barn. Lucy and Peanut, the two horses left behind, were stretching their necks over the corral fence.

When Skye saw Chad, every fiber of her being wanted to run into his arms and give him a great big hug. It wasn't just his dimples and his brown eyes with long curly eyelashes that Skye admired, or even his blond curls that peaked out of his black Stetson. Besides his dreamy looks, Chad Dressler was the coolest Christian guy Skye had ever met, and if Skye wasn't so young, she'd believe in her heart that she loved him. But for now, he was just one of her best friends, someone with whom she could share her deepest cares. So, until they were both old enough to date—and Chad said they would—Skye was perfectly content to call him "friend."

Mrs. Chambers and Skye jumped out of the truck as Chad and the two dogs hurried toward them. On the driver's side, Mr. Chambers got out of the truck, retrieved Morgan's wheelchair from the cab, and steadied it on the driveway in front of the barn. He then gently transferred Morgan from the truck to the chair.

"Chad!" Skye yelled, "I have so much to tell you!" The dogs squealed and wiggled, vying for any attention they could get.

"Hi, Chad!" Mr. Chambers and Morgan yelled from the far side of the truck.

"Hi, guys!" Chad said, then gave Mrs. Chambers and Skye a warm embrace. "Man, it's great to see you all. And, Skye, ever since you mentioned your dad on the phone the other night, I could hardly wait to hear the whole story."

Gulp! Skye's face turned red hot and her heart did back flips. *My "friend" Chad just gave me a hug. This moment will be cherished forever!* She quickly reached down to pet the dogs. "I met an aunt in Charleston that I didn't even know I had," she said as she stared into Chad's gorgeous eyes. "Her name's Millie Eister and she told me all about my dad. His name is Jacy Nicholson. Then we drove to Gatlinburg and found him. We spent all day yesterday with him and his wife, Ruth."

"I think Skye was ready to stay with them," Morgan piped in.

"Nah," Skye said, "but it was great getting to know my dad." *Now, why would Morgan say something like that?* "Chad, he and Ruth are Christians!"

"Hold on a minute, honey," Mrs. Chambers said to Skye, fussing over the dogs. "You'll have plenty of time later to fill him in on all the details. Chad, it's good to see you. Anything new around here?"

Mr. Chambers rushed to Chad's side and shook his hand. "Well, well, how's our house-sitter doing? Were you bored to death for the last few weeks?"

Chad released a hearty laugh. "Mr. C, you've got to be kidding. Two horses to ride, two dogs to play hide-and-seek with, a pool table, and three computers with scads of video games and you're wondering if I was bored? This place is a teen's paradise."

Morgan wheeled herself next to Mrs. Chambers. The dogs rushed toward her, greeting her with squeals and tail wags. She reached down and pet the dogs. "Well, I'm glad to be home."

"Welcome home, Morgan!" Chad gave Morgan a welcome hug.

"Did you take good care of Lucy and Peanut?"

Chad poked his Stetson back off his forehead and punched his thumb over his shoulder. "Those two horses were treated like royalty. I rode them every day, brushed their coats until they sparkled, and gave them double oats. I think they'll be sorry you guys came home."

Everyone laughed as Mr. Chambers said, "Did anything happen since we called you this morning, or is all well?"

Chad blew on his fingernails and then squared his Stetson. "Everything is A-OK. This place ran like a well-oiled machine. Oh, two more customers called. They're crying the hard-drive-crash blues. And, Mrs. C., Sherry Watson called from the town library and wanted to know if you'd serve on some kind of committee this coming school year. Other than that, things were hot, humid, and in slow motion as they usually are in the summer around here."

"Well, down south," Skye said, "it was hot and humid, but everything was in fast motion, and my head's still spinning. I can't wait to tell you all I learned about my real dad."

"And wait until you see all the ribbons we won in the horse shows," Morgan said.

She keeps changing the subject, Skye reasoned.

"I've got all night," Chad said. "Skye, how about filling me in over a game of pool?"

Mr. Chambers patted Skye on the shoulder. "First we have to bed down the horses, grab a quick bite, and unpack."

"I'll be glad to help any way I can," Chad said with his heart-stopping smile.

"After we get settled in," Mrs. Chambers said with a smirk, "Skye's all yours."

And I'd love to be yours, Skye dreamed, *now and forever.*

Motor-mouth-Skye told Chad every detail of her three-week trip, including meeting her Aunt Millie and her dad and how she felt about the whole thing. But her rambling didn't stop with Chad.

Every chance she had for the next few weeks, she told everyone she met about her southern adventure and how her real dad was now part of her life. At church, especially with the Youth for Truth teen group, Skye filled in all of her friends about what had happened, and they were all glad for her.

But deep inside Skye's heart was the nagging realization that her real mother was still missing. Other than having her personal information already listed on the family and friends search engine, Skye had no idea how to track down her mother. Also, she was still baffled over Morgan's ups and downs. As soon as she had a free moment, Skye planned to have another heart-to-heart talk with the one girl who had always been there for her when she needed help. Now, Skye figured, it was time to try to return the favor.

"Mom," Skye said to Mrs. Chambers during family devotions in the living room one night, "I think God led us to Aunt Millie and my dad, don't you?"

"Absolutely," Mrs. Chambers said.

"It was no mistake," Mr. Chambers said, smoothing his mustache then flipping some pages in his Bible. "God had every little detail of our trip to Charleston planned."

"That's one thing I love about God," Morgan said. "He has all our paths laid out, and if we follow him, we'll follow the right path, and life will be much easier."

"Listen to this verse," Mr. Chambers said as he pointed to a page in his Bible. "Matthew 21:22 says, 'If you believe, you will receive whatever you ask for in prayer.' Skye, we know you've been praying to find your parents for a long time. I believe in God's perfect time, he'll lead you to your mother just like he did your father. Just keep praying."

"And, Skye," Morgan said, "didn't you memorize a really neat verse from Jeremiah for Bible school a few weeks ago? Where's that verse and how does it go? Something about our plans ..."

Skye stared at the wall and then recited the verse from memory. "Oh, I remember. It's Jeremiah 29:11: 'For I know the plans I have for you,' declares the Lord, 'plans to prosper you and not harm you, plans to give you hope and a future.' That verse sure sounds to me as though all this parent business in my life right now is no accident."

"Well, Skye," Mrs. Chambers said, "if you've done all you can to find your mother, then from that point on, you just wait on the Lord."

Staring into space, Morgan spoke in a whisper, almost as though she were thinking out loud. "Maybe someday I'll find my father, too."

"Whenever God feels that you're ready, I think he'll bring that to pass," Mr. Chambers said.

"There's not much else I could do to find my mother," Skye said. "With her name changed, it seems almost impossible to find her. Maybe she's looking for me, too, but nothing's ever turned up on the locator website. I check it every day."

"Lately I've been thinking about plugging my name and my dad's in that website, too," Morgan said to Mr. and Mrs. Chambers. "Maybe we could connect again."

"Go right ahead," Mr. Chambers said. "That would be wonderful if you could track him down, too. Girls, just remember nothing's impossible with God."

"Could we pray together about our parents right now?" Skye asked.

"Sure," Mrs. Chambers said. "Just open your heart to God, girls. He's ready and willing to help the both of you. "

"Dear God …" Skye said, and started the family in a special prayer time.

The summer rolled on with autumn fast approaching, and Skye prayed faithfully as she emailed Millie and IM'd Emma and her father every day. "Father," she had told Jacy she'd call him. "I know that sounds a little stuffy, but I can't keep two 'Dads' straight in my brain." Without fail, she also called her father and Ruth once a week, and they shared the latest in their lives with each other.

Skye desperately wanted her new family to see where she lived, so plans were made for a special family gathering at Keystone Stables. With Denny's first extended leave coming over the Labor Day weekend, Millie suggested that they all come to Pennsylvania then. Jacy and Ruth agreed and told Skye that nothing short of an earthquake or the Lord's return would keep them from coming, too. Skye thought she never could be so excited over anything in her life again until she received an awesome phone call from Millie right before supper on the last Saturday of July.

R-r-ring!

Skye put her job of setting the dining room table on hold and answered the phone. Mrs. Chambers and Morgan were busy working on a chicken casserole in the adjacent kitchen, and Mr. Chambers was putting in some extra hours in his computer fix-it shop in the basement.

"Hello, Chambers residence. Skye speaking."

"Skye, this is Aunt Millie."

"Hi, Aunt Millie. You're calling me a day early. What's up?"

"Skye, I have the best news you'd ever want to hear. Your mother just called me."

"What?" Skye screeched and chills ran up and down her spine. She held the phone away from her mouth and yelled toward the kitchen. "Mom, Millie heard from my real mother!"

At the stove, Mrs. Chambers turned and gave Skye a beaming smile. "That's wonderful, Skye."

"Cool," was Morgan's curt reply as she chopped fresh broccoli at the counter.

"Aunt Millie," Skye practically yelled into the phone, "did you tell her about me? Where does she live? Is she okay? What's her new name? Can I—"

"Slow down, Skye," Millie said. "Now just pull up a chair, have a seat, and listen. I'll tell you everything she told me. Are you ready?" Millie chuckled.

"I've never been more ready in my whole life," Skye said. "Go ahead. Shoot."

chapter twelve

Skye pulled out a chair and sat at the dining room table. She was convinced that if she didn't, her wobbly knees would land her flat on the floor. "Aunt Millie, go ahead," Skye practically yelled. "Tell me what's happening."

In the kitchen, Mrs. Chambers and Morgan worked in silence, listening.

"Skye," Millie said, "this is unbelievable. Your mom has wanted to contact you—and me—for years, but she didn't know how to do that and still keep out of sight from Jacy. She's not computer savvy, so several years ago, she had a friend go on the same website as you did, but she had plugged in her new name with some scanty information. And it must have been before you entered your information, so she didn't find you. Of course, nothing ever came of it—until last week when she had someone check again and there you were. When had you put your information on that website?"

"Just a few weeks ago," Skye said. "And after we met you, I entered you, too. You mean she found me on that search engine?"

"Yes," Millie said. "Since you had entered my name, e-mail, and phone number as your contact, she called me. With my crazy schedule, she was trying for well over a week. When she finally did get through to me, she said she didn't want to leave a message because she wanted to make sure this was all legit, and that Jacy wasn't behind a big scam to track her down. Skye, when I told her how I met you in June, she almost went nuts. She said she lives every day with the torture of giving you up so long ago, and she'd give anything to see you."

"Where does she live? When can I meet her?"

"Hold on now," Millie said. "As much as she wants to see you, there are some conditions."

"Conditions?" Skye couldn't believe what she had just heard. "What do you mean?"

"Skye, I tried to explain to her how you found Jacy in Gatlinburg and how he's turned his life around and how me and him have been in touch, but she's still running scared. She still doesn't want him to know where she is."

"But he's a Christian now," Skye said. "He wants to make things right."

"I told your mom that," Millie said. "I even told her how he's married again and he's holding a steady job and all, but—well—she's just not ready to accept it yet."

"So what do I have to do to talk with her? To meet her?"

"Skye, she wants you to call her on her cell phone, but under no circumstances are you to give that number to your father. Do you understand?"

"Sure, but—"

"And one other thing," Millie added. "When you do contact her, she wants you to call her 'Rita.' She's not willing to tell us her new name or where she lives or any-thing like that yet. It's unreal, but after all these years, she's still pretty shook up over what happened between her and Jacy. It's really too bad."

"When can I call her?" Skye asked, her whole body quivering.

"She said the best time is after nine p.m. during any weekday. She didn't tell me why, and I didn't ask. She said I can call her anytime, too, so I plan to do that a lot. Maybe we can convince her that your father *is* a different man."

"Did she say anything about whether she's married or has other kids or anything like that?"

"Nope," Millie said. "We talked for only a few minutes because she said she had an appointment or something. But she did say over and over again that she wants to talk to you. Do you have a paper to write down her number?"

"Wait a sec." Skye pivoted to a counter and grabbed a notepad and pencil. "Okay, go ahead."

"Now remember, Skye. Under no circumstances are you to give this number to your father. Rita made me promise within an inch of losing my hide that I wouldn't tell Jacy she called me. I'm pretty sure she'll do the same with you. She says she changes cell phone numbers almost as often as she changes clothes, and she threatened to do it again if she has any inkling that Jacy got a hold of this number."

Skye said goodbye to Millie and waved the paper in the air as she rushed toward Mrs. Chambers. "Mom, I can call my mother! Millie gave me her phone number!"

"That's wonderful, Skye." While stirring a casserole bubbling in a large pan, Mrs. Chambers turned and smiled at Skye. "What are the *conditions* you were talking about?"

In silence, Morgan placed napkins and silverware on her lap, wheeled past Skye and started working on four place settings.

Skye moved out of Morgan's way and rambled on. "My mother wants me to call her 'Rita,' so she knows it's me calling her. No one else knows her by that name.

Aunt Millie said I'm not to even think about giving this number to Dad, and I'm to call *Rita* after nine p.m. any weekday. I have to wait two whole days!"

"That's my girl," Mrs. Chambers joked. "As patient as a new-born filly waiting for its first meal from its mother."

Skye turned and looked at busy Morgan, who was still strangely silent. "Morgan, what do you think of this great news?"

"It's great, Skye," Morgan said as though she struggled to get it out. "Really great."

Okay, Skye told herself, *this has gone on long enough. I've got to get to the bottom of this—and now.* Parking her thoughts about her mother somewhere in the back of her brain, Skye concentrated on Morgan. Skye strolled to the sliding glass door and placed her hands on her hips. She drank in the beautiful scene before her: a red barn, six horses grazing in a pasture surrounded by a white fence, a crystal blue sky, and a gentle summer breeze. "Wow, will you look at this gorgeous day? Perfect for a ride."

"Sure is," Mrs. Chambers agreed.

"Morgan," Skye said, "after supper why don't we ride out to Piney Hollow? That is, if Mom doesn't need us for anything around here." She shifted her gaze to Mrs. Chambers.

"The evening's yours," Mrs. Chambers said, scooping the casserole into a large serving dish. "Tom and I have big plans. We're going to catch up on some reading and bill paying. Later he wants to watch a ball game on TV. How exciting is that for two *old* folks on a Saturday night?" Mrs. Chambers laughed.

"Aw, Mom, you guys aren't that ancient—but just about," Skye kidded and then asked Morgan, "How about that ride, Sis?"

"Sure." Morgan giggled. "Blaze and I would love to double date with you and Champ."

"Well then it's settled." Mrs. Chambers placed the casserole in the center of the table. "After we clean up the dishes, you girls may go riding off into the sunset. Now, Skye, would you please go call the man of the house? Supper's ready."

"Sure." Skye headed toward the basement door.

"And I'll get the lemonade." Morgan wheeled toward the refrigerator.

"It's a great day to go riding off into the sunset," Skye said as she opened the basement door and headed down the stairs, "with my best bud and my favorite horse."

With a little more than two hours of perfect daylight left, Skye and Morgan rode their horses through the woods to Piney Hollow.

Riding side by side on the dirt road, the girls talked about everything and anything, about boys, about their trip south, about the upcoming school year, and then about their families. Skye figured the timing was perfect to ask Morgan about her feelings and what seemed to be bugging her.

"Morgan, I've noticed that you're always wound up in a tight little ball whenever I talk about my real family," Skye said. "I thought we had that all settled. I told you I'm not leaving my home here. As far as I'm concerned, you are my sister with a capital 'S' and you always will be."

The usually bubbly Morgan said nothing. For several moments, only squeaking saddles, chirping birds, and a buzzing fly filled the silent void.

"Morgan," Skye pleaded, "this isn't your style. As long as I've known you, you've been on top of things, encouraging me. You've always been like a light bulb in a pitch-black room to everyone who knows you. What gives?" She noticed tears rolling down Morgan's cheeks.

Morgan quickly brushed them away, almost as though she was embarrassed that anyone would ever see her cry.

Skye didn't quite know what to say next. *Wow! Something's really got her bugged. God, please help me with this one.*

"Is it something I've done—or said?" Skye asked. "Please tell—"

"Skye, it's nothing you've done," Morgan said. "It's me."

"What do you mean?" Skye asked as the girls rode into the Piney Hollow campsite. Again, Morgan was silent.

For just a moment, Skye darted her glance from Morgan to the fantastic view that lay straight ahead, one of her favorite spots in the world.

The girls rode to the outdoor chapel and stopped not far from the cross. Since Morgan had no way of dismounting, Skye decided to stay on Champ as well. "Let's just hang out here for a few minutes," Skye said, turning Champ to face Morgan and Blaze. Skye chewed her lip and leaned her forearm on the saddle horn, contemplating what she could say to get Morgan to spill her guts.

"Skye," Morgan finally said, "I've been watching you through this whole business with your parents, and I've discovered something about myself that I don't like very much."

"Oh?" Skye said. "What's that?"

"Well ..." Morgan wiped her eyes and gave Skye one of those radiant smiles that had been scarce for most of the summer. "... I think I'm angry at my parents for abandoning me. I never admitted it before, but I think I am."

"You? Angry at anyone? That's a joke," Skye said.

"No, really. I've noticed how anxious you are to know your parents, even after everything that's happened to you, and I've been checking my attitude, and it's not even miles close to yours. I haven't always cared whether or not I saw my mom or dad. And yet, deep down in my heart, I miss them and want to be with them. I think

85

God's been trying to get my attention through you. I really haven't done anything to try and keep in touch with my mom—or to find my dad, and lately I feel terrible about the whole thing."

"But you've always told me that your dad went to California and has never contacted you since he left. I remember you telling me how hard it is to get hold of your mom. Doesn't she move a lot? And she doesn't exactly call you every week either."

"I've been losing some sleep over that lately, too," Morgan said. "She moves so much I can't keep track of where she is, but she always stays within earshot of my Aunt Martha in Philly. Sometimes it seems to me that Mom's running from something. And as far as her keeping in touch with me—well—maybe it's because of the way I treat her that she doesn't come around more often. I always figured she had three other kids and she didn't want me, so I just kinda dropped her like a hot potato. All I ever needed to do was call Aunt Martha if I really wanted to keep in touch with Mom. I'm sure Mom has sensed how I've felt. I think God's not too happy at all about my real-family situation."

"But didn't you just tell us that you plugged your dad's name into that locator website?"

"Skye, that's the first time I ever did anything to try to track him down. Lately, I just feel horrible about everything."

Skye thought for a moment and then asked, "Well, why didn't you say something before about all of this? I mean, I thought you were always one happy camper here. No pun intended."

"Double duh!" Morgan poked her index finger in her cheek and made a face at Skye. "It's easy to push something to the back burner when you really want to. But with you and your parents being the hot topic in every discussion lately, the real-family blues came crashing down on top of me and started staring me right between the eyes. I haven't been able to get Mom or Dad out of my mind for weeks now."

"Morgan, what's your mom like?"

"She's kinda roly-poly, and she has dark hair, that is, when she's not bleaching it blonde or red. When we get back to the house, I'll show you a few pictures of her that I stashed away in my room. All I ever remember her doing was washing clothes and cooking for us four kids. She never laughed much, I guess, because she was always so busy with the housework and everything. I did what I could to help with the three younger kids, but how much can a twelve-year-old do in a wheelchair? When Dad left Mom had to get a job, so we kids went to stay with Aunt Martha some evenings and Saturdays. When Mom found out that Dad wasn't going to send any child support, she had to do something to get me help. That's when she gave me the choice to go to a facility or go into foster care."

"That must have been awful."

"It was. I kinda understood about Mom and how hard everything was for her, but I still felt abandoned." She sniffed back a tear. "I mean, I can't even begin to tell you how bad it hurt. You hear people talk about broken hearts, but it felt just like that, you know? Like a knife in my chest."

"Why didn't you live with your aunt?"

"Aunt Martha?" Morgan sneered. "If you knew *gorgeous blonde* Aunt Martha, you wouldn't even ask. She's never been married and has a big fancy job as a hotshot publicist with the Coilco Oil Company. She travels all the time. She could hardly handle the times we hung out at her place for a few hours while Mom worked. There's no way she'd get pinned down with someone like me."

"What's your dad like?" Skye asked.

"The last time I saw him he was built a lot like Mr. C. Dad had always shaved his head because he was losing his hair, and he said he hated his receding hairline. He was never around much when he lived at home with Mom and us kids. He was either working two jobs or hanging out at the bowling alley or golf club."

"Does he have red hair?"

"No, his hair was brown—when he had some. He said my red hair came from one of the grandparents, but I'm not sure which one. Skye, the more I think about my parents, the more I miss them." Once again, Morgan's eyes grew red and moist.

"Remember what Dad—ah, Dad Chambers—said the other night in devotions about God being in all of this?"

"Yep."

"And remember that God knows how you feel, and he's going to help you."

"Sure, I know that," Morgan said. "I've asked him to forgive me, and I really do want to touch base with my folks again. I really do."

"Don't you think God knows that?" Skye bobbed on Champ's back as he stomped away a fly. "As long as we do what's right, God will do the rest."

"I guess so," Morgan said, brushing a fly off Blaze's neck. "I'd really like to connect with my parents again, and God knows that."

"Then why don't you start tonight?" Skye asked. "Let's go back to the house and you can give your mom a call. What are you waiting for?"

"You're right, Skye," Morgan said. "I'll do it tonight."

he number you have dialed is no longer in service ...

Saturday night Morgan came up dry trying to reach her mother, and every time she tried to call her aunt, she got another recorded message asking the caller to leave a phone number. "Maybe Aunt Martha's on one of her cruises again," she said to Skye. "I guess I'll have to play the waiting game."

But the story was different for Skye. On Monday evening at nine o'clock sharp, Skye, with jittery hands, punched in her mother's cell phone number. Mr. and Mrs. Chambers and Morgan sat at the dining room table giving Skye moral support.

"Hello." A woman's gruff voice on the phone spoke with an air of suspicion.

"Is-is this Rita?" Skye's nerves had already gotten the best of her.

"Who's this?" the voice asked.

"Th-this is Skye Nicholson, and I'd like to speak to Rita, please." Skye's voice squeaked.

"Skye? Is this my baby Skye?" Without another word, the woman started weeping uncontrollably. "Sk-Skye—" she tried to speak, but nothing came out but sobs.

Skye found herself in a stranglehold of emotion matching that of her long-lost mother. Just as when Skye met her father, her often-suppressed feelings came bursting through. Her face turned red hot and her eyes burned with a sudden flood of tears that trickled down her face. "R—Rita, ma'am, are—are you okay?" Skye riveted on Mrs. Chambers, whose eyes were also red as she gave a smile and a reassuring nod.

Mr. Chambers reached to the counter, grabbed a tissue and handed it to Skye. Morgan focused on Skye with genuine interest.

"Thanks," Skye whispered to Mr. Chambers and dabbed her eyes. "Rita?" she said into the phone.

"Yes, Skye baby," the woman said. "I'm here. I'm so glad you called. Your father's not with you, is he?"

"No, ma'am," Skye answered. "He's in Gatlinburg. I'm in Pennsylvania with my foster parents and foster sister."

Skye heard her mother sniffle and blow her nose before she spoke again. "I told Millie I don't want him to know where I am. I hope she told you that."

"She did, but he's different now. He wants to talk to you and tell you he's not after you anymore. He's married to a nice lady, and he has a whole new life."

"Well, that's nifty for him, but he doesn't need to talk to me. Let's just let it go at that," Rita said. "So you're at your foster home right now?"

"Yes, I am," Skye said. "Where do you live?"

"I'd rather not say at the moment. But I will tell you that I'm in Pennsylvania. And you said you're in Pennsylvania? So that means we're close enough that we could meet?"

"Yes," Skye said. "I'd really like to."

"I hope so," Rita said. "And I do want to see you as soon as possible. I've agonized all these years wondering where you were, and—" Again, Rita began to weep.

Skye held the phone away from her mouth and whispered to Mr. and Mrs. Chambers. "She lives somewhere in Pennsylvania and she wants to see me ASAP. What should I tell her?"

Mrs. Chambers whispered back, "You two make plans, and we'll take you wherever you need to go."

"R—Rita," Skye said, "I can meet you anytime you want. Do you want to come here?"

"I—I'd rather not," Rita said, regaining her composure. "I'd like to meet in some neutral place. Maybe we can have a picnic at a park or something."

"Will anyone be with you?" Skye asked. "I mean, do you have a family?"

"I'll be coming alone," Rita sniffled. "I have—well— I'll be coming alone."

Wow, she really doesn't trust anyone, Skye figured. "I'll be coming with my foster family, but if you want to see me by myself, they can sit in the truck or go to a picnic table nearby." Skye glanced at Mrs. Chambers who nodded and smiled.

"No, that's all right, Skye," Rita said. "I'd like to meet the family you live with now. Really."

Skye whispered to the Chambers, "She wants to meet all of us at a park somewhere for a picnic."

Mr. Chambers nodded and gave Skye a thumbs-up.

"That'll be fine with us," Skye said.

Rita paused then said, "Skye, do you know where Matunga State Park is? It's on route 83, about halfway between Harrisburg and the Maryland border."

"Yes," Skye said. "That's one of my favorite places in the whole wide world. We've camped there and have walked the falls and everything."

"Well," Rita said, "are you able to meet me there this Saturday? I don't have to work."

"She wants to meet us at the Matunga State Park this Saturday," Skye whispered, and everyone nodded.

"Yes, ma'am. We can be there," Skye told Rita. "Where should we meet you—and what time?"

"Can you meet me at the picnic tables by the bridge near the falls at eleven?" Rita asked.

"Yes," Skye said.

Mr. Chambers gave Skye another nod and a smile.

"I'll wear a bright red shirt so you can't miss me. How does that all sound?"

"I'll wear a red top too," Skye said.

"Don't worry, baby," Rita said. "There's no way I'm going to miss you on Saturday. I've been missing you all these years, and it's finally going to end. I can't wait to hold you in my arms again."

"Yes, ma'am." Skye beamed a radiant smile. "We'll be there at eleven sharp."

Right after her phone conversation with Rita, Skye searched through her dresser and closet and decided that her cherry red T-shirt would probably be red enough to wear. But when modeling it for Mrs. Chambers and Morgan, Skye kidded that she still needed neon strips and a string of glowing lights sewn on the shirt to make sure her mother would see her.

"I have no doubt your mother will see you," Morgan said. "No doubt at all."

The week dragged on so slowly, Skye began to think she was in some kind of science fiction nightmare where time-warp aliens tortured the earthling teens by morphing every second into an hour. All week long, Skye kept gawking at her watch, hoping with her whole heart that it would suddenly become Saturday at 11 a.m.

Finally, Saturday morning did arrive in a hot and humid package, and at 11:03 am the Chambers family pulled into the parking lot adjoining the picnic pavilions at the Matunga State Park.

"Wow," Skye said, "look how full it is!"

"I'm not surprised," Mrs. Chambers said. "School starts in a few weeks, so everyone's trying to get their last-minute summer fun in."

Her chest booming, Skye rolled down the cab window, stretched her neck, and scanned the row of picnic tables along the road. As Mr. Chambers parked the truck in one of the few open stalls, Skye's glance darted wildly, examining every pavilion and table for the color red. Mrs. Chambers and Morgan were doing the same. Skye spotted several red shirts, but children claimed them all.

"I hope she's already here," Morgan said. "As jam packed as this place is, I bet there aren't any tables left."

"We might have to eat lunch in the truck," Mr. Chambers said to his wife. "But your ham salad sandwiches would even taste good in the barn! It doesn't matter to me where we eat them."

Skye had no interest in food whatsoever. "Can we get out and look?"

"Of course," Mrs. Chambers said. "Tom, try to find an empty—"

"Over there!" Skye yelled. "Look! At the table next to the wooden bridge! I see a plump lady in a red shirt and blue jeans. It looks like she has long, dark hair, and she has it pulled up into some kind of twisted knob. She's sitting at a table by herself, and her back's to us. I bet she's doing that because she's still running scared."

"I see her," Mrs. Chambers said. "You might be right, Skye. She probably doesn't want to be facing all these people."

"That must be her!" Skye opened the door and jumped out. "Let's go!"

"Just hang on a minute," Mrs. Chambers said, getting out of the car. "We'll all go together. Wait until Tom gets Morgan into her chair."

Skye did double time raking her hands through her hair and chewing her lip. "Okay, okay, what can I do to get us there faster?"

"Nothing, Skye," Mr. Chambers said. "We'll leave the cooler in the back of the truck until later." Mr. Chambers hopped out of the truck and retrieved Morgan's wheelchair from the back of the cab. "If that woman isn't your mother, we'll grab the nearest vacant table." He set the chair firmly on the macadam pathway and placed Morgan in it.

"Thanks, Mr. C.," Morgan said then she glanced at Skye and giggled. "Why, Sis, your face is as red as that shirt. You're not too excited, are you?"

Focused on the stranger, Skye had completely tuned out the last few seconds of conversation. She turned, reached behind the cab, and lifted the cooler out of the flatbed.

"Skye," Mr. Chambers said. "We're not taking that with us now. You have enough on your mind."

Skye turned and started hurrying toward the bridge. "Let's go," she said again. Glancing back, she gestured for her family to hurry. "C'mon."

Mrs. Chambers started pushing Morgan toward the bridge and chuckled. "Something tells me Skye wants us to follow her."

"Let's go, Mr. and Mrs. C.," Morgan said. "That girl is going absolutely bonkers."

Skye had trouble keeping her legs from running full speed ahead toward the bridge. She glanced back, reassuring herself that the rest of her family was following as best as they could. But just several yards from her goal,

Skye came to an abrupt stop. Huffing, she studied the woman's hair, trying its best to beat the humidity and stay in its disheveled knob. Skye's glance drifted to the woman's broad back, blotches of perspiration soaking through the bright red shirt. *I don't want to scare her,* she reasoned as she wiped beads of sweat from her own forehead. Again, she glanced at Mr. and Mrs. Chambers and Morgan and waited as they came by her side.

"Go ahead," Mrs. Chambers said, smiling.

Skye turned and, again, studied the woman who sat facing the other way, waiting. *What if it isn't my mother?* Skye thought. *This could all be a big mistake.*

Finally, Skye took a deep jagged breath and spoke her mother's real name. "Rita?"

The woman stood, and with tears streaming down her fiery red face, looked in Skye's direction.

While Skye stared at the stranger, the woman's expression suddenly melded into shock and disbelief, and her face turned pale as a whitewashed fence.

"R–Rita?" Skye asked. "Are you my mother?"

Then Skye heard Morgan shrieking beside her. "Mom? What are you doing here?"

"Mom? Where's your mom?" Skye spun toward Morgan; then quickly surveyed the grounds for another woman, but there was no one.

"Mrs. *Hendricks*?" Skye heard Mrs. Chamber's voice as if it were coming from far away. *"You're Rita?"*

"What's going on?" Skye demanded of the stranger. "Are you my mother?"

chapter fourteen

Skye glanced at Mr. and Mrs. Chambers standing with their faces locked in complete confusion. Skye stared at Rita who could do nothing but return an astonished look.

"She's *my* mother, Nancy Hendricks!" Morgan exclaimed. "But—how—this can't be for real. How can you be Skye's mother when you're my mother?"

Skye felt like she had been wrapped in duct tape with only her lungs and brain able to function, and they were barreling full speed ahead. Finally, she managed to speak as she focused on Rita. "Now wait. You're my mother ... and you're Morgan's mother too? Is that what I'm hearing? You've got to be kidding!" Skye glanced at Morgan, whose face was still draped in disbelief, and then she shifted back to Rita who just sat and stared.

Mr. Chambers made his way to the picnic table. "Folks, it seems as though we have one of the world's greatest mysteries right before our very eyes." He released a nervous smile as he lifted his Stetson, scratched his head, and carefully squared his hat. "Let's try to relax and sort this all out."

Skye positioned Morgan in her wheelchair next to a corner of the table, but couldn't find one word to say.

"Well, this is certainly one for the books." Mrs. Chambers shook the woman's hand and spoke with a quivering voice. "It's good to see you again, Nancy. Should I assume correctly that you are also Rita, Skye's mother?"

Prodded by Mrs. Chambers, Rita shook her hand and then flopped back onto the bench. As her gaze darted from Skye to Morgan and back, she nervously chewed her lip. "I—I don't know what to say. I don't know where to begin. This is unbelievable. The last time I visited Keystone Stables, I didn't see Skye there."

"She wasn't with us then," Mr. Chambers said. "She came several months later."

"Morgan never mentioned Skye in any of her phone calls," Rita said.

"You mean all two of them?" Morgan's voice portrayed total embarrassment.

Rita dabbed her eyes and blew her nose in a tissue. "And last Monday evening when I talked with Skye, I never asked her anything about her foster parents. So I had no way of knowing."

Skye was still unable to move.

"Skye," Mrs. Chambers said, "earth to Skye." She hurried to Skye's side, wrapping her arm around her shoulders. "C'mon, honey. We'll get this all sorted out."

Following her lead, Skye approached the table. As she did, Rita rushed toward Skye and drew her into a warm embrace. "Skye," the woman wept uncontrollably, "I'm so sorry about everything."

Slowly Skye wrapped her arms around the chubby woman's frame and rested her head on Rita's chest drenched with perspiration. Despite the confusion running through her mind, Skye felt strangely complete as she finally connected with the woman who had given her life. At last, Skye felt that she was home.

With deep sobs, Rita tried to speak as she hugged Skye tightly. Moving her to arm's length, she moaned, "My baby Skye."

After another long tearful embrace, Rita turned toward Morgan. "Morgan," she said, "I really don't know where to begin telling you how sorry I am about—everything." She bent down and gave Morgan an enormous hug. "I really am very glad to see you. How have you been?

Suddenly, tough girl Skye found herself sniffling back a barrage of tears as she focused on Morgan, whose eyes were also red and moist.

"Well, Mother," Morgan cried, "I'd be lying if I told you I've been fine."

Rita backed away and studied Morgan intently. "What do you mean? Are you sick or something? What's the matter?"

"Nothing like that," Morgan said, wiping tears from her face. "I've just been missing you lately, that's all."

"I know I haven't acted like it, but you've never been out of my thoughts." Rita gave Morgan another hug and stepped back to the table. "I guess I have a lot of explaining to do." The woman dabbed her face, red and blotchy from the sweat and tears.

Skye quickly brushed away her own tears and forced out a smile. "Start at the beginning," she said.

"Yes, we have all day," Mr. Chambers said, sitting on the bench.

Mrs. Chambers sat on the opposite side of the table from Rita and gestured to Skye. "C'mon, honey, sit down and get comfortable."

Skye joined Mrs. Chambers at the table, folded her hands to stop them from quivering, and riveted her attention on her real mother.

"I'm sure Rita—ah—Nancy—ah—" Mrs. Chambers paused. "What would you like us to call you?"

For a moment, Rita stared into space. "Skye can decide what she'd like to call me. If she likes 'Mom' or 'Mother,' that's fine with me."

"And I'll just keep calling you Mom," Morgan said with a slight chuckle. "Why change now?"

"The other day I told Millie on the phone that everyone should call me Rita, but with this latest development, I think it would be best if you call me Nancy. That's been my name for the last eleven years, so let's just stay with that and forget Rita."

"Fine," Mr. Chambers said.

"Nancy," Mrs. Chambers said, "why don't you start by telling us what happened after Jacy went to prison."

Nancy took a deep jagged breath and began. "When Jacy threatened to kill me, the police helped me change my identity. That's when I left Skye with Millie. Giving up Skye was one of the hardest things I've ever done." With her bottom lip quivering, Nancy glanced at Skye and released another barrage of tears. "Within a year I moved back to the Scranton area with my new name, Nancy McMillan, and a new hair color." She tugged at a few strands of straggly hair dangling in front of her ear.

Skye studied her brand-new mother and started comparing the woman's looks to her own. *Our eyes are the same, and so is our hair, that is, if that's her natural color.*

"Skye," Nancy said, "I'm not dyeing my hair anymore. Our hair color's the same."

"And our eyes," Skye said with a tearful smile.

Nancy continued, "After working at a bookstore in Scranton for a few months, I met Mike Hendricks, a book distributor. His wife had just died of kidney failure, and he was caring for his four-year-old daughter by himself." Nancy looked in Morgan's direction and smiled. Then she slipped off the bench and knelt beside Morgan, embracing her hands. "Morgan, I'm so sorry, but I have another bombshell for you. You were that little girl. You're Mike's daughter, not mine. You were too little at that time to know that. When Mike and I got married, I was thrilled that I could take care of you because I was still grieving over giving up Skye. Please forgive me for not telling you before. Please!" Nancy sobbed.

"You mean you're just my stepmother?" Morgan gasped as her eyes grew big and her eyebrows peaked.

"Morgan, I loved you as my own daughter," Nancy said. "And then when the other three kids came along, it never seemed that important anymore to tell you. You all got along so well."

"So my real mother died?" Morgan's look of disbelief deepened.

"Yes," Nancy wailed, wiping her cheeks. "And I'm begging you to forgive me for not telling you before. Oh, everything is such a mess."

"Wow!" Morgan cried as she wiped her face of a flood of tears as well. "This *is* a biggie. And I thought it was Skye's big day! It's going to take a while for all of this to sink in."

"It's going to take a while for all of us to process this." With tear-filled eyes, Mrs. Chambers grasped Skye's hand. "But I believe God has allowed all of this to happen for a purpose. It seems that the truth needs to come out—and now. I believe the girls want to try to accept anything you have to tell them, Nancy."

"I am." Morgan stared deep into her stepmother's eyes. "But I'm not sure if knowing the truth about my real mother when I was younger would have made any difference with the way I feel now. I love you as my real mother. My problem is that I haven't shown it lately."

Nancy gave Morgan a reassuring smile and said, "I know you were terribly hurt when I had to put you into foster care. It hurt me deeply, too. That was also one of the hardest things I've ever done. In fact, I had to live over that same hurt that I suffered when I had to give Skye to Millie. That's why I haven't called or visited more. It seems like I've gained a reputation for giving kids away. That's not at all the way I planned my life to be."

"Nancy, we don't hold that against you, and neither does God." By now, Mr. Chambers had also joined the tear fest. "Sometimes life dishes out some awfully painful experiences. But as Eileen said before, God has it all worked out for everyone's best interest."

"I sure hope so," Nancy said, sniffling.

"Morgan has told me a lot about her brother and two sisters," Skye said. "So that means they're mine, too."

"Well, they'd be your half siblings," Nancy said. She slipped back onto the bench. "There's Stevie, and he's nine. Then there's Tasha, who's seven, and Richelle, who's just five. Today they're with my husband's sister, Martha. I brought a whole bunch of pictures with me, if you'd like to see them later." Nancy smiled at Morgan. "Have you told them about Aunt Martha?"

"Yeah," Morgan said, dabbing at her eyes, "and I'm surprised she's not fluttering around Europe or someplace like that right now."

"It's one of her rare times at home," Nancy said. "I wasn't sure if I should bring the other kids. I didn't know how you'd feel about them, Skye. If I would have only known."

"Don't worry about that," Mrs. Chambers said. "We'll meet them in good time."

Skye glanced at Morgan and released a super smile. "I'm sure if those kids are anything like my best friend, they're cool. I can't wait to meet them."

"It's still hard to believe that you're not my real mother," Morgan said, "and as far as I'm concerned, it really doesn't matter. Honest it doesn't. But the more I think about things you did in the past, the more they make sense now. So how are the little rascals? Lately I've really been missing them."

"They're all doing pretty good," Nancy said. "It's tough trying to raise them and keep a full-time job. Your father hadn't sent any child support for years, but just over the last few months, he's started sending some checks. That money helps a lot."

"So you know where he is?" Morgan asked.

"Yes," Nancy said. "He's still in California."

"I'd like to write to him," Morgan said. "I'd love if he could tell me about my real mother. Can I have his address?"

"Sure thing," Nancy said. "I'm sure he'd love to hear from you. I think he's mellowed a bit as he's grown older. He often asks how you are."

"Nancy—" Skye started and then said, "Mother ... do you mind if I call you that?"

"I'd love if you would," Nancy said.

"That way I can keep you and Mom Chambers straight." She glanced at Mrs. Chambers, who gave her that same reassuring smile, and then looked at her real mom again. "Mother, I met Father several months ago and we keep in touch all the time now. You don't need to hide from him anymore. He became a Christian, and he's told me again and again that the car accident was all his fault. He's not out to get you, and he just wishes you the best. He wants me to try to convince you of that."

"I've been watching my back all these years," Nancy said, "and it's kinda hard believing someone can change just like that."

"So that's why you were always dyeing your hair different colors and asking Dad to move all the time," Morgan said. "Now this is all starting to make sense. I always wondered why you seemed scared of something and not totally happy."

"Yes," Nancy said, staring at the table. "We've moved more times than I care to count. But the last few years I've stayed in the Philly area within close reach of Martha."

Mr. Chambers finished his water and set the bottle on the table. "Nancy, we've all met Jacy, and he really is sincere. He has a lovely place in Gatlinburg, and he's married a wonderful Christian woman. Both are involved in a local church. Christ has changed his life. The only reason he wants to see you again is to ask you to forgive him."

"Mother," Skye pleaded with Nancy. "Won't you please meet with him? For me?"

"I'll think on it," Nancy said unconvincingly. "That's all I can do right now. I'll think on it."

During a ham salad picnic that extended well into the afternoon, the Chambers' family and Nancy shared their lives. Skye looked at dozens of pictures of Nancy's three other children and Morgan in her younger days. In return, Skye told her mother everything she could remember about her last eleven years, including the bad foster homes as well as the good ones. Morgan, having come to grips with the fact that Nancy was her stepmother, joined in wholeheartedly. When Millie's name came up, the girls recounted their trip down south, how they met Millie, and the plans that Millie had made to come to Pennsylvania over the Labor Day weekend.

"Mother," Skye said, "why don't you and the kids come to Keystone Stables the same weekend?"

"Yeah," Morgan added. "We have enough bedrooms for all of you, don't we, Mrs. C.?"

"Sure," Mrs. Chambers said. "We have lots of room."

"Oh, I'd love to see Millie and the kids again. I plan to keep in touch with her on the phone, but my heart yearns to see her. And I'd love to spend some time with both you girls."

"At Keystone, we have a picnic grove, and a campsite, and six horses and everything," Skye said. "The kids will have a blast. Dad, we could have a cookout at Piney Hollow, couldn't we?"

"We sure can," Mr. Chambers said, "that is, if it's not raining."

"What's Piney Hollow?" Nancy asked.

Morgan's freckled face lit up with her signature smile. "It's a campground with a chuck wagon in the back section of Keystone Stables. The kids will love it. We can have roast hot dogs and marshmallows and have a scavenger hunt."

"Well, that sounds wonderful," Nancy said. "I can take a four-day weekend. The factory usually gives us a holiday on Labor Day anyway. I'll take Friday off, too, and we'll drive to Keystone Stables then. How does that sound?"

"Super!" Skye said then asked Morgan, "What do you think, Sis?" Skye glanced to her side and stared at Morgan in a whole new light. *Wow! She really is my sister, three times over: stepsister, foster sister, and sister in Christ.*

"Double super!" Morgan said. "I can't wait."

In the late afternoon, Skye waved goodbye to Nancy one last time and settled into her seat in the back of the truck.

As they pulled away from the picnic grove, Mrs. Chambers looked in the rearview mirror. "Skye, I noticed that you didn't tell your mother that Jacy and Ruth are planning to visit us then, too. Have they changed their minds?"

Mr. Chambers looked in the rear view mirror at Skye. "I was wondering about that, too, Skye. What's the story?"

"Yeah." Morgan poked Skye in her arm. "What gives?"

Skye blew out a long sigh. "Oh, they're still coming, and—well—I have a plan."

"A plan?" Morgan asked. "Look out, world! When Skye Nicholson has a plan, things usually start happening—and fast."

"What's the plan, Skye?" Mrs. Chambers asked.

"I figured that Mother would want to head for Alaska if she knew Father was coming to Pennsylvania, so I didn't want to tell her yet. I'm thinking that as I call her a few times a week all summer long and get to know her better, she'll accept what I've told her about him. Then, a few days before the Labor Day weekend, I'll tell her he's coming, too."

"I see," Mrs. Chambers said. "You're taking a big risk, Skye."

"And, Skye," Mr. Chambers said, "even if your mother does agree to see him, I have a feeling that she won't stay under the same roof overnight, even though our house is plenty big."

"I've thought about that, too," Skye said. "Since Moyers' Bed and Breakfast is right down the road, I'll ask Father if he and Ruth would mind staying there."

"Hmm," Mr. Chambers said. "Now think this through, Skye. If your scheme doesn't pan out, and your mother feels that you aren't being totally honest with her, she might get very angry. The whole situation could blow up in your face and damage the relationship you just started."

"But if she just gives Father a chance, and she sees how he's changed, she'll be glad that she was able to see him again," Skye said.

"I'm with you," Morgan said. "From what I remember, Mom's always been scared of her own shadow, and she got much worse after my dad left and she was on her own. I think it's a great idea to try to have Jacy and her connect. She'd finally stop watching her back all the time."

"Are you going to tell your father about your scheme?" Mr. Chambers asked Skye.

"Oh, yes," Skye said. "I think he'll go for it. He told me he's willing to do anything to talk with Mother and get things right. I'm sure he'll still want to come."

"So, how are you going to plan their meeting?" Mrs. Chambers asked.

"Well," Skye answered, "if Mother and the kids come on Friday, we could have a picnic at the gazebo on Saturday afternoon. I'll ask Father if he could arrive around noon then. That way we'd all be together, including Millie and her kids, when Father and Ruth get there. We can all give Mother moral support. I also thought it would be nice to have Chad come to the picnic, too."

"Skye, you are one riot." Morgan giggled. "What does Chad have to do with your parents and their reunion?"

"Well—"

Mrs. Chambers winked at Morgan then turned to Skye. "Of course we need Chad there. How else will we know how many burgers to grill? Right, Skye?"

Mr. Chambers joined in the fun. "Morgan, it's common knowledge that Skye can't do a thing without Chad's approval. Everybody knows he's her activities director."

"Aw, Dad." Skye's red-hot cheeks were not from a sunburn.

"Putting all jokes aside," Mr. Chambers said, "Skye, if you think this plan will work, then go for it, but we all need to put a lot of prayer behind it. I know you desperately want peace in your family, even though your parents aren't together anymore."

"Having Mother know that Father's a decent man means a whole lot to me," Skye said. "I want to drift off to sleep every night not having to worry about them anymore."

"I feel the same way about the whole situation, too," Morgan said.

"Then let's go for it!" Skye said.

appy trails to you, until we meet again ...."

Under a rippling pink sunset as soft as angels' wings, Skye's and Morgan's "two families" sat around a campfire on Friday evening of the Labor Day weekend. After Mr. Chambers' hot dog and baked potato supper, everyone joined in a round of western songs and silly choruses while they roasted marshmallows. With September's crisp evening air inviting jackets, the crackling fire added the final touch to a chuck wagon cookout nestled in the shadows of the three Piney Hollow hills.

Skye's excitement level shot up, and she could focus on nothing but getting to know her family better. She glanced at her mother and smiled, receiving an apprehensive smile in return. After some fancy convincing on Skye's part, her mother had agreed to see Jacy the next day. But now a discreet look of worry on Nancy's face overshadowed all the fun. *Lord,* Skye prayed, *help her to know tomorrow will all work out.*

Skye found herself so consumed with her thoughts, she forgot about three marshmallows on her stick and sent the black gooey globs oozing to their doom into the dancing flames. Private Dennis Eister, United States Marine Corps, sitting with his mother on the other side of the circle, came to the rescue.

"Skye, give me your stick," he said, standing and reaching toward Skye. "At the rate you're going, we'll be out of marshmallows in five minutes! I'll do some for you. How do you like them?"

"Burnt to a crisp," Skye said.

Dennis gave Skye a snappy salute "At your service, ma'am." He grabbed three marshmallows from the bag on the table, stuck them on Skye's stick, and went to work.

While Dennis gave his "mallow duty" everything he had, Skye gazed at the handsome blue-eyed young man in USMC T-shirt and black shorts. His muscles bulged like a pro wrestler's, his blond hair was shaved "high and tight," and his frame bore a bronze tan, a telltale sign of the summer he had just spent training in the southern heat. *Morgan was right*, Skye thought. *He is one handsome dude.*

Skye's gaze swept the circle and studied her new family, each face glowing with the warmth of the bed of hot embers. Deep down in Skye's heart, another warmth burned, one that matched the blazing flames. *Now when Chad and Father come tomorrow*, she mused, *the scene will be totally complete.*

Skye focused on her mother, trying her best to have a good time, who was busy mastering the marshmallow-roasting technique. She let out a round of chuckles as she pushed several rebel strands of hair behind her ear, touched a brown lump on the end of her stick, and then yanked her hand away. "Girls, I'm about ready to hire Dennis myself. If this gooey mess wasn't so good, I'd give it up and go drink coffee."

"Aw, Mom," Morgan giggled, "part of the fun is seeing who can keep the little white puffs on their sticks long enough to toast them just right and then rescue them before they slide off into the fire. I've only lost one so far."

Skye glanced at Morgan, to her mother's left. With her beaming freckled smile, Morgan was showing Richelle how to hold the stick. The little girl, a miniature version of her mother, left no room to doubt whose daughter she was. *And she looks just like me with Aunt Millie in that ancient picture*, Skye thought. *How cool is that?*

Next to Morgan sat tomboy Tasha, tall and lanky with glasses, blonde hair drawn back into a ponytail, having the time of her life wrestling with her food and yelling at her "all boy" brother, Stevie. With a barrage of giggles, he poked Tasha with one hand and poked his stick at the embers with the other, sending crackling sparks twirling into the air. "He looks just like my dad," Morgan had told Skye, "only he has enough hair to part, and his belly's not quite there yet."

On the other side of the campfire sat Aunt Millie, whom Skye had grown to love and admire. Skye knew Millie sometimes had two or three part-time jobs to make ends meet. Because Millie had instilled a dogged work ethic in her two kids, Dennis had a bright career ahead of him in the Marines, and Emma was heading for college in another year. *All they need is Jesus*, Skye thought, *and they'll make it big time.*

Completing the circle, the Chambers' two Westies, Tippy and Tyler, sat panting and waiting for a morsel from Mrs. Chambers who sat holding a stick with four toasted marshmallows.

"Tom," she said, pivoting toward Mr. Chambers who was pouring lemonade and iced tea into paper cups at the table, "you better come get these before they turn into charcoal."

Mr. Chambers hurried to his wife and slid the marshmallows off the stick and onto a paper plate. "I've learned my lesson," he said. "These babies will sit and cool for a few seconds before I indulge. I don't need scorched fingers or a burnt tongue."

Skye studied her foster parents as they talked and laughed and thoroughly enjoyed each other's company. Mrs. Chambers, with her beautiful blue eyes and Mr. Chambers always squaring his cowboy hat and smoothing his mustache, were a special couple, Skye concluded. After helping dozens of kids over their fifteen or so years together, they still loved kids, and each other. *I owe them oodles*, Skye told herself. *Maybe someday I can get married to a wonderful guy, and we can help kids too. I know that would make Mom and Dad Chambers happier than anything else in the world.*

"Skye!" Her mother's voice brought Skye back to earth. "The kids haven't had so much fun in a long time. I just hope I can get past tomorrow, and we'll all be fine."

"Don't worry, Mother," Skye said. "I'm sure everything will be okay." *With Chad and Father here tomorrow, it sure will be okay!"*

The Saturday before Labor Day, the day for which Skye had prayed and waited, finally arrived! She could think of nothing that meant more to her than having both of her parents with her at the same time and smiling. *God,* she prayed on Friday night before bedtime, *please help Mother accept the truth tomorrow. If she sees how you changed Father and how you can change anyone, maybe she won't be scared of him anymore. Maybe she'll accept you into her life, too.*

Skye had no trouble getting up on a morning that brought sunshine, blue skies, and a gentle breeze. Before breakfast, she and Morgan had already hurried to the barn to feed and groom the horses and to get them ready for their big day. Of course, Skye shared all of her hopes and fears with Champ, who listened with nickers and nudges.

After the entire household indulged in Mr. Chambers' famous scrambled-egg breakfast, Skye and Morgan took Dennis, Emma, and Nancy's three kids to the field where six tacked horses waited. All morning Mr. and Mrs. Chambers, Nancy and Millie got ready for the picnic at the gazebo, and Skye and Morgan taught the kids horse care and gave riding lessons.

Morgan, sitting with Richelle on Blaze, instructed Stevie and Tasha how to neck-rein their mounts in the training corral. At the same time, Skye took Dennis and Emma on a lazy ride on trails that interlaced the Keystone Stables land. Although being with Champ was enough reason to go, Skye had an ulterior motive to have some time alone with her two cousins. Near mid-day, the three rode to the bottom of the large fenced-in field and stopped at the pond where the three horses, like nails to a magnet, were drawn to the succulent grasses along the water's edge.

For the entire ride, Skye had her eye on her watch, checking every few minutes in anticipation of her father's arrival. But now, she took a deep breath of the crisp, clean air, glanced at the cloudless azure sky, and soaked in the warmth of the sun's rays. As her gaze drifted to the horses, a breeze swept across the field, teasing tufts of the horses' manes and tails to whisk freely. Skye smiled at Dennis and Emma whose faces expressed nothing but pure delight. *Now's as good a time as any to talk to them about God*, Skye reasoned.

"Skye, this place is fantastic," Dennis said, his eyes taking in the scene before him.

"You are *so* lucky," Emma said. "I know a couple of foster kids, but I've never heard of anyone being in a foster home as neat as this one."

"I wouldn't exactly say that I've been lucky," Skye said as she stroked Champ's neck.

"What do you mean?" Emma's big brown eyes flashed with interest.

"Well," Skye said, "I've learned from the Bible that God has my life all planned out. It's no accident that I came here. You should've known me before Mom and Dad Chambers rescued me. I hung out with gangs and everything. The judge was ready to ship me to a detention center for lousy kids and throw away the key."

"That's hard to believe," Dennis said. "You just don't seem like the gangbanger type. What happened? Did Mr. and Mrs. Chambers lock you in your room for three months?" He let out a hearty laugh.

"Yeah, you just seem like a normal kid to me," Emma said.

Skye looked deep into her cousins' eyes. "After I moved in here, I was still a mess for a while. I pulled all kinds of stupid stunts, and I wanted to leave because Mom and Dad Chambers had a whole bunch of rules that I didn't like."

Dennis chuckled and saluted Skye. "You should visit a Marine training camp if you think you have rules here."

"Anyway," Skye continued, "the big change came in my whole attitude when I accepted Christ. Mom Chambers told me that I'd never make it in life without having Jesus in control. I finally had to accept the fact that I was a rotten kid, and only God could clean me up. I couldn't do it on my own."

Deep in thought, Dennis rubbed his chin. "You know, Mom always watches TV programs on Sunday morning that talk about the same thing—about being saved and stuff like that. But we've never gone to church. It hasn't been important to us. Now you've got me thinking, Skye. I've always felt like something's been missing in my life but I don't know what. Maybe it has something to do with God."

Emma also had a faraway look. "Skye, it's really strange that you're telling us all of this. Bonnie, one of my friends at school, is always razzing on me to go to church with her. She's tried to explain about Jesus and all that stuff, but I could never quite get the hang of what she was saying. Maybe I'll tune in better the next time the subject comes up."

"There was so much that I never understood until Mom Chambers took the time to explain everything," Skye said. "When we die, we're going to live somewhere forever, and we can't get to heaven just by trying to be good. It's only by accepting Christ as our Savior that we'll get there."

"That's the same thing Bonnie's always telling me," Emma said.

"Interesting philosophy you have there, Skye," Dennis said as he brushed a horsefly off his horse's neck.

Skye gave her cousins a heartfelt smile. "The Keystone Stables family always goes to church on Sunday. Would you like to go with us tomorrow? We have a super teen group called Youth for Truth. I'd love if you'd meet all my friends. I want to show off my new family."

"Hmm, church," Dennis said. "I'm for far-out experiences. Sure. Why not?"

"You've got me thinking, too," Emma said to Skye. "I'd really like to know more about this God business. I guess now's as good a time as any."

"Skye," Emma said, "what do you think is going to happen when your mom sees your dad today?"

"I've been thinking about that a lot, too," Dennis said. "This could be a disaster."

"Well," Skye said, "I've been hoping and praying for this day my whole life. I just have to believe that everything will turn out all right. It's just gotta."

"I sure hope you're right," Dennis said."

"We're rooting for you," Emma added.

Skye glanced at her watch for the umpteenth time and then looked across the field to the barn. Mr. Chambers, in his towering chef's hat, was helping Morgan and the younger children dismount. Down the walkway from the back of the house came Chad, and Skye's heart did its usual back flip.

"C'mon," Skye said to her cousins, neck-reining Champ to her right. She gently dug her heels into his belly, nudging him forward. "It's 11:30 already and just about time for lunch and the biggest family reunion of my life."

chapter sixteen

H i, Chad," Skye said, her heart racing like a grey-
hound after a rabbit.

"What's up, Skye?" Chad's dimples flashed
his gorgeous smile. Leaning against the fence, he looked
sharp in his black Stetson, red-checkered shirt, jeans, and
black boots.

Morgan sped off on her Jazzy toward the gazebo. "I
hear the picnic table calling me!" she yelled back. "See
you guys later!"

"I guess you've met my two little sisters and brother."
Skye said to Chad as she pointed to the three younger
children who were watching Mr. Chambers tether the
horses in the corral.

"Yeah," Chad said. "Mr. C. just introduced us. That
is too cool, Skye."

Skye slipped off Champ and tied him next to the other
horses. Dennis and Emma followed suit with their mounts.

"Chad, these are my cousins from Charleston, Dennis
and Emma Eister."

"Hi," Dennis said, giving Chad a warm handshake.

"Hi, Chad. We've heard *a lot* about you." Emma
slipped Skye a "gotcha!" smile.

For once, it was Chad, not Skye, whose face suddenly looked sunburned.

"Emma, sh-h," Skye whispered.

"Chad is Skye's activities director," Mr. Chambers joked, starting toward the gazebo. "Isn't that right, Skye?"

"D-a-ad!" Skye said as she parked her hands on her hips.

"Well, it's the truth," Mr. Chambers said then turned to the younger children. "C'mon, kids. Lots of picnic fun awaits you."

"What's an activities director?" Tasha asked as the three children started to follow Mr. Chambers.

"You dumb girls don't know anything." Stevie ran past his sisters to catch up with Mr. Chambers. "He directs her activities. Anybody would know that."

Mr. Chambers suddenly stopped, pulled a spatula from his back pocket and raised it like a general uplifting his sword as he prepared for battle. "On to bigger and *burger* things. Charge!" He gently grasped Richelle's hand and started toward the gazebo with Stevie and Tasha giggling and romping by his side.

"That man's out of his tree." Dennis laughed, crawling between the fence rails to join Chad.

"There's never a dull minute around here," Emma said. "I'm beginning to see that big time."

"Shall we?" Chad took off his Stetson and held it over his heart, bowing before Skye and Emma. "Ladies first."

"Oh, Chad, you're too much." Skye giggled as she and Emma joined the boys and the four headed off to the gazebo.

After the picnickers grilled a few dozen burgers, sliced a watermelon, spilled a super-size bag of chips all over the table, and poured a dozen drinks in large red plastic cups, they sat at the table, and Mr. Chambers prayed. While the families chatted and ate more than they ever intended, Skye kept her focus on the parking lot next to the house.

At 12:16, a tan SUV crept into Keystone Stables and pulled in next to Millie's white Tracker.

He's here! Skye almost said out loud. She glanced at her mother, busy cleaning up Richelle's spilled drink and not noticing the incoming car. Skye glanced at Morgan, who gave her a thumbs up, then she shifted to Mom and Dad Chambers, who both nodded, their signal for Skye to go greet her very special guests.

"I'll be right back," Skye said to anyone who cared to listen. She hurried to the parking lot and greeted her father and Ruth with generous hugs. A sweet waft of Canoe shaving lotion permeated the air, mellowing the tension Skye had built up within her senses.

"Mother and the three kids are over at the gazebo," Skye said, pointing.

Skye's father took a long deep breath and ran his hand over his thin hair. "Skye, Ruth and I been praying about this moment ever since you suggested it. This might be the answer to your mother's terrible fear of me."

Ruth took her husband's hand. "Hon, I'm sure she'll be all right once you talk with her. What happened between you two was a lifetime ago."

Skye chewed her lip, glanced at the gazebo and finally said, "Are you ready?"

"Let's do it." Skye's father managed a weak smile as he slipped his hand around Skye's.

Slowly, the three walked toward the gazebo.

"I've been practicing all week what I want to say to her," Skye's father said. "I sure hope she'll listen."

Skye focused on Mom and Dad Chambers who stood and faced her, blocking Nancy's view. Skye shifted her glance beyond her foster parents to her mother, still busy with spills and her squirming children's demands. At the other end of the table Chad, Morgan, Millie, Dennis, and Emma sat in silence, chewing slowly, waiting for the awkward "reunion."

Mr. Chambers reached his hand toward Skye's father. "How are you?"

"I think I'm fine." Skye's father shook Mr. Chambers' hand.

"Ruth, it's good to see you again," Mrs. Chambers said, shaking the woman's hand.

"It's good to see you," Ruth said nervously.

"Mother," Skye said to Nancy as Mr. and Mrs. Chambers stepped aside, "Father's here."

"What's that?" Nancy said. Still busy with the spill, she smiled as she turned toward Skye.

"Hello, Rita," Jacy said.

Nancy glared at her ex-husband and, trying to process the whole situation, her beet-red face melded into pure distress.

Skye remembered the same look before, the day she and her mother had met. "Mother, please sit down and talk so you two can get things ironed out," she pleaded.

For a moment, no one said a word.

"Mom, who's that man?" Stevie asked, pulling at his mother's arm.

"Th-this is Skye's daddy, honey," Skye's mother stuttered. "R-remember, I told you he might be here today?"

"Rita," Jacy said. "I've been looking for you for a long time, and I—"

"This wasn't my idea, you know." Skye's mother's lips quivered. "Just stay your distance, Jacy, and I'll be fine." She edged her body away from the bench and stood with her arms crossed, just staring.

"Rita, I just want to say I'm sorry for everything that's happened." With an outreached hand, Skye's father took one step forward.

Skye's mother took several steps backward.

No one at the table moved.

Mrs. Chambers rushed to Nancy's side and slipped her arm around her shoulders. "Nancy, Skye planned this meeting to make things right between you and Jacy, not to frighten you."

Skye rushed to her mother's other side, urging her to calm down. "Mother, I need you to see that Father is different—really different."

Skye's father took another step forward, then stopped. "Rita, or should I say 'Nancy,' I've cleaned up my life and I'm not full of hate and revenge anymore." He gave Ruth a nervous smile. "This is my wife, Ruth. We have a new life in Christ and with each other. I just needed to see you to tell you that. You can stop running."

For a moment, nothing stirred but a napkin that fluttered away in a sudden fickle breeze. The tense scene holding the picnickers captive had even filtered down to the youngest as the three children sat staring at their mother.

Skye looked deep into her mother's frightened eyes. "Mother, please listen. Father's telling the truth. I want you to be at peace. Nothing would make me happier. Please. I love you. I love you both." Tentatively, Skye grasped her mother's hand.

Suddenly, Nancy started to weep. Skye felt her mother's heart and soul open up and her body relax as the woman released eleven years of fear and desperation. She cried and cried.

"It's okay, Mother," Skye said as she patted her on the back. "We're all here for you."

Mrs. Chambers grabbed a napkin from the table and handed it to Nancy. "It's all right, Nancy. There's no reason to be afraid anymore."

"What's the matter, Mommy?" Richelle asked as she stared at her mother. "You're cwying."

"Mom?" Tasha and Stevie said almost in unison.

"I'm okay," Nancy sniffled as she reached and touched her children's shoulders. "There's nothing to worry about." She dabbed her face with the napkin.

"Why don't we all sit down," Mr. Chambers said, returning to his seat.

Mrs. Chambers joined her husband. "Nancy, do you mind if Jacy and Ruth join us?"

Eyes filling with tears, Skye prodded her mother toward the bench. "C'mon, Mother. Let's sit down."

Morgan motored next to her stepmother. "Mom," she said with her eyes also full of tears, "this is all for the best. Please try to relax."

"All right," Skye's mother cried. Still focused on her ex-husband, she slipped back to her seat between Stevie and Tasha, picked up Richelle, and positioned her on her lap. "I don't know if I'm ready for all of this."

While Morgan returned to her spot, Skye quickly slipped next to Tasha, folded her hands to steady them, and shifted her glance around the table.

"Nancy," Millie reached and touched the woman's arm, "we haven't been a real family for all these years. Let's try to put the past behind us and make amends—for the kids' sakes."

Nancy dabbed her eyes, her glance darting around the table. She took a deep jagged breath and drew Richelle in a close embrace. Stevie and Tasha stared at Jacy and Ruth who sat next to Mr. Chambers.

"Nancy, please," Skye's father said.

"I—I'll give it a try," she said, "but it will take some time."

Suddenly, a gentle breeze seemed to usher in a sense of calm. Skye, once a tough gangbanger now a softhearted Christian, brushed a flood of tears from her cheeks as she studied the entire scene.

Thank you, God, Skye prayed as she glanced at Mom and Dad Chambers who were looking back, both with moist eyes. Skye shifted to her father and Ruth who, with pleading looks, sat staring at Skye's mother. Next sat Morgan, Millie, Emma, and Dennis who dared to release stingy smiles. Then there was Chad.

Skye focused on the special young man who was staring back with a brand new look, one of the deepest respect and care. Even in the shade of his Stetson, his curly eyelashes enhanced a sparkle in his eyes as he gave Skye a smile. "Skye," he said, "you've done it again. You never cease to amaze me. You're quite a gal."

"I'll say amen to that," Mr. Chambers said.

"I've watched Skye learn to rely on God," Mrs. Chambers said. "And we know that with God, all things are possible."

"Well, I've seen the impossible happen right here today," Dennis said. "This is unbelievable."

"Mom, can I have another hot dog?" Stevie asked while he and Tasha worked on a handful of chips. Richelle, her head resting against her mother's chest, had no interest in food.

"I'm so glad we came," Millie said.

"And I'm so glad we're all together," Morgan said. "Today is a day that I'm sure none of us will ever forget. I know that I won't."

"And who knows what the future might hold. Right, Skye?" Chad said.

"Right!" Skye said as she again gazed into the eyes of one of her dearest friends in the whole wide world. Then she shot a quick glance toward the barn, where Champ stood tethered to the corral. With her beloved horse and the family she loved all together on a beautiful September day, Skye sent up a short grateful prayer. *Thank you, God. I owe it all to you.*

Chad flashed back his dimples, tipped his hat and gave Skye a wink that she knew she'd never, ever forget.

"All I can say is this whole situation has been a God thing," Skye beamed. "Our God is the best ever." Again, she looked around the table, took another quick glance at Champ, and then gave Chad her very best smile.

A Letter to my Keystone Stables Fans

Dear Reader,

Are you crazy about horses like I am? Are you fortunate enough to have a horse now, or are you dreaming about the day when you will have one of your very own?

I've been crazy about horses ever since I can remember. When I was a child, I lived where I couldn't have a horse. Even if I had lived in the country, my folks didn't have the money to buy me a horse. So, as I grew up in a small coal town in central Pennsylvania, I dreamed about horses and collected horse pictures and horse models. I drew horse pictures and wrote horse stories, and I read every horse book I could get my hands on.

For Christmas when I was ten, I received a leather-fringed western jacket and a cowgirl hat. Weather permitting, I wore them when I walked to and from school. On the way, I imagined that I was riding a gleaming white steed into a world of mountain trails and forest paths.

Occasionally, during the summer, my mother took me to a riding academy where I rode a horse for one hour at a time. I always rubbed my hands (and hard!) on my mount before we left the ranch. For the rest of the day I tried not to wash my hands so I could smell the horse and remember the great time I had. Of course, I never could sit at the dinner table without Mother first sending me to the faucet to get rid of that "awful stench."

To get my own horse, I had to wait until I grew up, married, and bought a home in the country with enough land for a barn and a pasture. Moon Doggie, my very first horse, was a handsome brown and white pinto Welsh Mountain Pony. Many other equines came to live at our place where, in later years, my husband and I also opened our hearts to foster kids who needed a caring home. Most of the kids loved the horses as much as I did.

Although owning horses and rearing foster kids are now in my past, I fondly remember my favorite steed, who has long since passed from the scene. Rex, part Quarter Horse and part Tennessee Walker, was a 14 ½ hands-high bay. Rex was the kind of horse every kid dreams about. With a smooth walking gait, he gave me a thrilling ride every time I climbed into the saddle. Yet, he was so gentle, a young child could sit confidently on his back. Rex loved sugar cubes and nuzzled my pockets to find them. When cleaning his hooves, all I had to do was touch the target leg, and he lifted his hoof into my waiting hands. Rex was my special horse, and although he died at the ripe old age of twenty-five many years ago, I still miss him.

If you have a horse now or just dream about the day when you will, I beg you to do all you can to learn how to treat with tender love and respect one of God's most beautiful creatures. Horses make wonderful pets, but they require much more attention than a dog or a cat. For their loyal devotion to you, they only ask that you love them in return with the proper food, a clean barn, and the best of care.

Rex

Although Skye and Champ's story that you just read is fiction, the following pages contain horse facts that any horse lover will enjoy. It is my desire that these pages will help you to either care for your own horse better now or prepare you for that moment when you'll be able to throw your arms around that one special horse of your dreams that you can call your very own.

Happy riding!
Marsha Hubler

Are You Ready to Own Your First Horse?

The most exciting moment in any horse lover's life is to look into the eyes of a horse she can call her very own. No matter how old you are when you buy your first horse, it's hard to match the thrill of climbing onto his back and taking that first ride on a woodsy trail or dusty road that winds through open fields. A well-trained mount will give you a special friendship and years of pleasure as you learn to work with him and become a confident equestrian team.

But owning a horse involves much more than hopping on his back, racing him into a lather of sweat, and putting him back in his stall until you're ready to ride him again.

If you have your own horse now, you've already realized that caring for a horse takes a great amount of time and money. Besides feeding him twice a day, you must also groom him, clean his stall, "pick" his hooves, and have a farrier (a horseshoe maker and applier) and veterinarian make regular visits.

If you don't own a horse and you are begging your parents to buy one, please realize that you can't keep the horse in your garage and just feed him grass cuttings left over from a mowed lawn. It is a sad fact that too many neglected horses have ended up in rescue shelters after well-meaning families did not know how to properly care for their steeds.

If you feel that you are ready to have your own horse, please take time to answer the following questions. If you say yes to all of them, then you are well on your way to being the proud owner of your very own mount.

1. Do you have the money to purchase:

   - the horse? (A good grade horse can start at $800. Registered breeds can run into the thousands.)
   - a saddle, pad, and bridle, and a winter blanket or raincoat? ($300+ brand new)
   - a hard hat (helmet) and riding boots? ($150+)
   - essentials such as coat and hoof conditioner, bug repellent, electric clipper and grooming kit, saddle soap, First Aid kit, and vitamins? ($150+)

2. Does your family own at least a one-stall shed or barn and at least two acres of grass (enough pasture for one horse) to provide adequate grazing for your horse during warm months? If not, do you have the money to regularly purchase quality oats and alfalfa/timothy hay, and do you have the place to store the hay? Oh, and let's not forget the constant supply of sawdust or straw you need for stall bedding!

3. Are you ready to get up early enough every day to give your horse a bucket of fresh water, feed him a coffee can full of oats and one or two sections of clean dry hay (if you have no pasture), and "muck out" the manure from the barn?

4. Every evening, are you again ready to water and feed your horse, clean the barn, groom him, and pick his hooves?
5. Will you ride him at least twice a week, weather permitting?
6. If the answer to any of the above questions is no, then does your family have the money to purchase a horse and board him at a nearby stable? (Boarding fees can run as high as a car payment. Ask your parents how much that is.)

So, there you have the bare facts about owning and caring for a horse. If you don't have your own horse yet, perhaps you'll do as I did when I was young: I read all the books I could about horses. I analyzed all the facts about the money and care needed to make a horse happy. Sad as it made me feel, I finally realized that I would have to wait until I was much older to assume such a great responsibility. And now years later, I can look back and say, "For the horse's sake, I'm very glad I did wait."

I hope you've made the decision to give your horse the best possible TLC that you can. That might mean improving his care now or waiting until you're older to get a horse of your own. Whatever you and your parents decide, please remember that the result of your efforts should be a happy horse. If that's the case, you will be happy too.

Let's Go Horse Shopping!

If you are like I was when I was younger, I dreamed of owning the most beautiful horse in the world. My dream horse, with his long-flowing mane and wavy tail dragging on the ground, would arch his neck and prance with only a touch of my hand on his withers or a gentle rub of my boot heel on his barrel. My dream horse was often different colors. Sometimes he was silvery white; other times he was jet black. He was often a pinto blend of the deepest chocolate browns, blacks, and whites. No matter what color he was, he always took me on a perfect ride, responding to my slightest commands.

When I was old enough to be responsible to care for my own steed, I already knew that the horse of my dreams was just that, the horse of my dreams. To own a prancing pure white stallion or a high-stepping coal-black mare, I would have to buy a Lipizzaner, American Saddle Horse, or an Andalusian. But those kinds of horses were either not for sale to a beginner with a tiny barn or they cost so much, I couldn't afford one. I was amazed to discover that there are about 350 different breeds of horses, and I had to look for a horse that was just right for me, possibly even a good grade horse (that means not registered) that was a safe mount. Color really didn't matter as long as the horse was healthy and gave a safe, comfortable ride. (But I'm not sure what my friends might have said if I had a purple horse. That certainly would have been a "horse of a different color!") Then I had to decide if I wanted to ride western or English style. Well, living in central Pennsylvania farm country with oodles of trails and dirt roads, the choice for me was simple: western.

I'm sure if you don't have your own horse yet, you've dreamed and thought a lot about what your first horse will be. Perhaps you've already had a horse, but now you're thinking of buying another one. What kind should you get?

Let's look at some of the breeds that are the most popular for both western and English riders today. We'll briefly trace a few breeds' roots and characteristics while you decide if that kind of horse might be the one for you. Please keep in mind that this information speaks to generalities of the breeds. If given the proper care and training, most any breeds of horses make excellent mounts as well.

Some Popular Breeds (Based on Body Confirmation)

The Arabian

Sometimes called "The China Doll of the Horse Kingdom," the Arabian is known as the most beautiful of horse breeds because of its delicate features. Although research indicates Arabians are the world's oldest and purest breed, it is not known whether they originated in Arabia. However, many Bible scholars believe that the first horse that God created in the Garden of Eden must have embodied the strength and beauty that we see in the Arabian horse of today. It is also believed that all other breeds descended from this gorgeous breed that has stamina as well as courage and intelligence.

A purebred Arabian has a height of only 14 or 15 hands, a graceful arch in his neck, and a high carriage in his tail. It is easy to identify one of these horses by examining his head. If you see a small, delicate "dish" face with a broad forehead and tiny muzzle, two ears that point inward and large eyes that are often ringed in black, you are probably looking at an Arabian. The breed comes in all colors, (including dappled and some paint), but if you run your finger against the grain of any pureblood Arabian's coat, you will see an underlying bed of black skin. Perhaps that's why whites are often called "grays."

Generally, Arabians are labeled spirited and skittish, even though they might have been well trained. If you have your heart set on buying an Arabian, make sure you first have the experience to handle a horse that, although he might be loyal, will also want to run with the wind.

The Morgan

The Morgan Horse, like a Quarter Horse (see below), can explode into a gallop for a short distance. The Morgan, with its short legs, muscles, and fox ears, also looks very much like the Quarter Horse. How can we tell the two breeds apart?

A Morgan is chunkier than a Quarter Horse, especially in his stout neck. His long, wavy tail often flows to the ground. His trot is quick and short and with such great stamina, he can trot all day long.

So where are the Morgan's roots?

The horse breed was named after Justin Morgan, a frail music teacher who lived in Vermont at the turn of the eighteenth century. Instead of receiving cash for a debt owed, Mr. Morgan was given two colts. The smallest one, which he called Figure, was an undersized dark bay with a black mane and tail. Mr. Morgan sold the one colt, but he kept Figure, which he thought was a cross between a Thoroughbred and an Arabian. Over the years, he found the horse to be strong enough to pull logs and fast enough to beat Thoroughbreds in one afternoon and eager to do it all over again the same day!

When Mr. Morgan died, his short but powerful horse was called "Justin Morgan" in honor of his owner. After that, all of Justin Morgan's foals were called Morgans. The first volume of the Morgan Horse Register was published in 1894. Since then, hundreds of thousands of Morgans have been registered.

If you go Morgan hunting, you will find the breed in any combination of blacks, browns, and whites. Don't look for a tall horse because all Morgans are between 14 and 15 hands tall, just right for beginners. If you're fortunate enough to find a well-trained Morgan, he'll give you years of pleasure whether you ask him to gallop down a country trail, pull a wagon, or learn to jump obstacles.

The Mustang

If you want a taste of America's Wild West from days gone by, then you should treat yourself to the "Wild Horse of America," the Mustang.

This 14–15 hand, stout horse has its roots from Cortez and the Spanish conquistadors from the sixteenth century. Although the Mustang's name comes from the Spanish word, *mesteno*, which means "a stray or wild grazer," he is most well known as the horse of the Native Americans. Numerous tribes all over the western plains captured horses that had escaped from their Spanish owners and ran wild. The Native Americans immediately claimed the Mustang as a gift from their gods and showed the world that the horse was, and is, easy to train once domesticated.

It didn't take long for the white settlers to discover the versatility of the Mustang. Because of his endurance, this little horse soon became a favorite for the Pony Express, the U.S. cavalry, cattle round-ups, and caravans.

Since the 1970s, the U.S. Bureau of Land Management has stepped in to save the Mustangs from extinction. As a result, herds of Mustangs still roam freely in U.S. western plains today. At different times of the year and in different parts of the country, the Adopt-a-Horse-or-Burro Program allows horse lovers to take a Mustang or burro home for a year and train it to be a reliable mount. After the year, the eligible family can receive a permanent ownership title from the government. As of October 2007, more than 218,000 wild horses and burros have been placed into private care since the adoption program began in 1973.

If you'd like a "different" kind of horse that sometimes has a scrubby look but performs with the fire of the Arab-barb blood, then go shopping for a Mustang. You'll find him in any black, brown, or white combination and with the determination and stamina to become your best equine friend.

The Quarter Horse

There's no horse lover anywhere in the world who hasn't heard of the American Quarter Horse. In fact, the Quarter Horse is probably the most popular breed in the United States today.

But what exactly is a Quarter Horse? Is he only a quarter of a horse in size, therefore, just a pony? No, this fantastic breed isn't a quarter of anything!

The Quarter Horse originated in American colonial times in Virginia when European settlers bred their stout English workhorses with the Native Americans' Mustangs. The result? A short-legged but muscular equine with a broad head and little "fox" ears, a horse that has great strength and speed.

It didn't take long for the colonists and Native Americans to discover that their new crossbreed was the fastest piece of horseflesh in the world for a quarter of a mile. Thus, the breed was christened the American Quarter Horse and began to flourish. Besides running quick races, it also pulled wagons, canal boats, and plows. When the American West opened up, cowpokes discovered that the Quarter Horse was perfect for herding cattle and to help rope steers. Although it remained a distinct breed for over three hundred years in the U.S., the Quarter Horse was only recognized with its own studbook in 1941.

If you are looking for a reliable mount that has a comfortable trot and smooth gallop, you might want to look at some *seasoned* Quarter Horses. (That means they have been trained properly and are at least five or six years old.) They come in any color or combination of colors. Their temperament is generally friendly, yet determined to get the job done that you ask them to do.

The Shetland Pony

Many beginning riders incorrectly believe that the smaller the horse, the easier it is to control him. You might be thinking, "I'm tiny, so I need a tiny horse!" But many beginners have found out the hard way that a Shetland Pony is sometimes no piece of cake.

Shetland Ponies originated as far back as the Bronze Age in the Shetland Isles, northeast of mainland Scotland.

Research has found that they are related to the ancient Scandinavian ponies. Shetland Ponies were first used for pulling carts, carrying peat and other items, and plowing farmland. Thousands of Shetlands also worked as "pit ponies," pulling coal carts in British mines in the mid–nineteenth century. The Shetland found its way at the same time to the United States when they were imported to also work in mines.

The American Shetland Pony Club was founded in 1888 as a registry to keep the pedigrees for all the Shetlands that were being imported from Europe at that time.

Shetlands are usually only 10.2 hands or shorter. They have a small head, sometimes with a dished face, big Bambi eyes, and small ears. The original breed has a short, muscular neck, stocky bodies, and short, strong legs. Shetlands can give you a bouncy ride because of their short broad backs and deep girths. These ponies have long thick manes and tails, and in winter climates their coats of any color can grow long and fuzzy.

If you decide you'd like to own a Shetland, spend a great deal of time looking for one that is mild mannered. Because of past years of hard labor, the breed now shows a dogged determination that often translates into stubbornness. So be careful, and don't fall for that sweet, fuzzy face without riding the pony several times before you buy him. You might get a wild, crazy ride from a "shortstuff" mount that you never bargained for!

The Tennessee Walking Horse

If you buy a Tennessee Walker, get ready for a thrilling ride as smooth as running water!

The Tennessee Walking Horse finds its roots in 1886 in Tennessee, when a Standardbred (a Morgan and Standardbred trotter cross) stallion named Black Allan refused to trot; instead, he chose to amble or "walk" fast. With effortless speed comparable to other horses' trots,

Black Allan's new gait (each hoof hitting the ground at a different time) amazed the horse world. Owners of Thoroughbreds and saddle horses were quick to breed their mares to this delightful new "rocking-horse" stud, and the Tennessee Walker was on its way to becoming one of the most popular breeds in the world. In just a few short years, the Walker became the favorite mount of not only circuit-riding preachers and plantation owners, but ladies riding sidesaddle as well.

Today the Walker, which comes in any black, brown, or white color or combination, is a versatile horse and is comfortable when ridden English or Western. He is usually 15 to 17 hands tall and has a long neck and sloping shoulders. His head is large but refined, and he has small ears. Because he has a short back, his running walk, for which he is known, comes naturally.

If you go shopping for a Tennesee Walker, you will find a horse that is usually mild mannered yet raring to go. Although most Walkers are big and you might need a stepstool to climb on one, you will be amazed at how smooth his walk and rocking-horse canter is. In fact, you might have trouble making yourself get off!

Some Popular Breeds (Based on Body Color)

The Appaloosa

French cave paintings thousands of years old have "spotted" horses among its subjects, ancient China had labeled their spotted horses as "heavenly," and Persians have called their spotted steeds "sacred." Yet the spotted Appaloosa breed that we know today is believed to have originated in the northwestern Native Americans tribe called the Nez Perce in the seventeenth century.

When colonists expanded the United States territory westward, they found a unique people who lived near the Palouse River (which runs from north central Idaho to the Snake River in southeast Washington State). The Nez Perce Indian tribe had bred a unique horse—red or blue roans with white spots on the rump. Fascinated, the colonists called the beautiful breed *palousey*, which means "the stream of the green meadows." Gradually, the name changed to *Appaloosa*.

The Nez Perce people lost most of their horses following the end of the Nez Perce War in 1877, and the breed started to decline for several decades. However, a small number of dedicated Appaloosa lovers kept the breed alive. Finally, a breed registry was formed in 1938. The Appaloosa was named the official state horse of Idaho in 1975.

If you decide to buy an Appaloosa, you'll own one of the most popular breeds in the United States today. It is best known as a stock horse used in a number of western riding events, but it's also seen in many other types of equestrian contests as well. So if you would like to ride English or Western, or want to show your horse or ride him on a mountain trail, an Appaloosa could be just the horse for you.

Appaloosas can be any solid base color, but the gorgeous blanket of spots that sometimes cover the entire horse identifies the special breed. Those spotted markings are not the same as pintos or the "dapple grays" and some other horse colors. For a horse to be registered as a pureblood Appaloosa, it also has to have striped hooves, white outer coat (sclera) encircling its brown or blue eyes, and mottled (spotted) skin around the eyes and lips. The Appaloosa is one of the few breeds to have skin mottling, and so this characteristic is a surefire way of identifying a true member of the breed.

In 1983, the Appaloosa Horse Club in America decided to limit the crossbreeding of Appaloosas to only three main confirmation breeds: the Arabian, the American Quarter Horse, and the Thoroughbred. Thus, the Appaloosa color breed also became a true confirmation breed as well.

If you want your neighbors to turn their heads your way when you ride past, then look for a well-trained Appaloosa. Most registered "Apps" are 15 hands or shorter but are full of muscle and loaded with spots. Sometimes, though, it takes several years for an Appaloosa's coat to mature to its full color. So if it's color you're looking for, shop for a seasoned App!

The Pinto

The American Pinto breed has its origins in the wild Mustang of the western plains. The seventeenth and eighteenth century Native Americans bred color into their "ponies," using them for warhorses and prizing those with the richest colors. When the "Westward Ho" pioneers captured wild Mustangs with flashy colors, they bred them to all different breeds of European stock horses. Thus, the Pinto has emerged as a color breed, which includes all different body shapes and sizes today.

The Pinto Horse Association of America was formed in 1956, although the bloodlines of many Pintos can be traced three or four generations before then. The association doesn't register Appaloosas, draft breeds, or horses with mule roots or characteristics. Today more than 100,000 Pintos are registered throughout the U.S., Canada, Europe, and Asia.

Pintos have a dark background with random patches of white and have two predominant color patterns:

1. Tobiano (Toe-bee-ah'-no) Pintos are white with large spots of brown or black color. Spots can cover much of the head, chest, flank, and rump, often including the tail. Legs are generally white, which makes the horse look like he's white with flowing spots of color. The white usually crosses the center of the back of the horse.

2. Overo (O-vair'-o) Pintos are colored horses with jagged white markings that originate on the animal's side or belly and spread toward the neck, tail, legs, and back. The deep, rich browns or blacks appear to frame the white. Thus, Overos often have dark backs and dark legs. Horses with bald or white faces are often Overos. Their splashy white markings on the rest of their body make round, lacy patterns.

Perhaps you've heard the term *paint* and wonder if that kind of horse is the same as a Pinto. Well, amazingly, the two are different breeds! A true Paint horse (registered by the American Paint Horse Association) must be bred from pureblood Paints, Quarter Horses, or Thoroughbreds. The difference in eligibility between the two registries has to do with the bloodlines of the horse, not its color or pattern.

So if you're shopping for a flashy mount and you don't care about a specific body type of horse, then set your sites on a Pinto or Paint. You might just find a well-trained registered or grade horse that has the crazy colors you've been dreaming about for a very long time!

The Palomino

No other color of horse will turn heads his way than the gorgeous golden Palomino. While the average person thinks the ideal color for a Palomino is like a shiny gold coin, the Palomino breed's registry allows all kinds of coat colors as long as the mane and tail are silvery white. A white blaze can be on the face but can't extend beyond the eyes. The Palomino can also have white stockings, but the white can't extend beyond the knees. Colors of Palominos can range from a deep, dark chocolate to an almost-white cremello. As far as body confirmation, four breeds are strongly represented in crossbreeding with the

Palomino today: the American Saddlebred, Tennessee Walker, Morgan, and Quarter Horse.

No one is sure where the Palomino came from, but it is believed that the horse came from Spain. An old legend says that Isabella, queen of Spain in the late fifteenth century, loved her golden horses so much she sent one stallion and five mares across the Atlantic to start thriving in the New World. Eventually those six horses lived in what is now Texas and New Mexico, where Native Americans captured the horses' offspring and incorporated them into their daily lives. From those six horses came all the Palominos in the United States, which proves how adaptable the breed is in different climates.

Today you can find Palominos all over the world and involved in all kinds of settings from jumping to ranching to rodeos. One of their most popular venues is pleasing crowds in parades, namely the Tournament of Roses Parade in Pasadena, California, every New Year's Day.

Perhaps you've dreamed of owning a horse that you could be proud of whether you are trail riding on a dirt road, showing in a western pleasure class, or strutting to the beat of a band in a parade. If that's the case, then the Palomino is the horse for you!

If you're shopping for the best in bloodlines, look for a horse that has a double registry! With papers that show the proper bloodlines, an Appaloosa Quarter Horse can be double registered. Perhaps you'd like a palomino Morgan or a pinto Tennessee Walker?

Who Can Ride a Horse?

As you have read this book about Skye, Morgan, and some of the other children with special needs, perhaps you could identify with one in particular. Do you have what society calls a handicap or disability? Do you use a wheelchair? Do you have any friends who are blind or have autism? Do you or your friends with special needs believe that none of you could ever ride a horse?

Although Keystone Stables is a fictitious place, there are real ranches and camps that connect horses with children just like Skye and Morgan, Sooze in book two, Tanya in book three, Jonathan in book four, Katie in book five, Joey in book six, and Wanda in book seven. That special kind of treatment and interaction has a long complicated name called Equine Facilitated Psychotherapy (EFP.)

EFP might include handling and grooming the horse, lunging, riding, or driving a horse-drawn cart. In an EFP program, a licensed mental health professional works together with a certified horse handler. Sometimes one EFP person can have the credentials for both. Whatever the case, the professionals are dedicated to helping both the child and the horse learn to work together as a team.

Children with autism benefit greatly because of therapeutic riding. Sometimes a child who has never been able to speak or "connect" with another person, even a parent, will bond with a horse in such a way that the child learns to relate to other people or starts to talk.

An author friend has told me of some of her family members who've had experience with horses and autistic children. They tell a story about a mute eight-year-old boy who was taking therapeutic treatment. One day as he was riding a well-trained mount that knew just what to do, the horse stopped for no reason and refused to budge. The leader said, "Walk on" and pulled on the halter, but the horse wouldn't move. The sidewalkers (people who help the child balance in the saddle) all did the same thing with the same result. Finally, the little boy who was still sitting on the horse shouted, "Walk on, Horsie!" The horse immediately obeyed.

So the good news for some horse-loving children who have serious health issues is that they might be able to work with horses. Many kids like Morgan, who has cerebral palsy, and blind Katie (book five) actually can learn to ride! That's because all over the world, people who love horses and children have started therapy riding academies to teach children with special needs how to ride and/or care for a horse. Highly trained horses and special equipment like high-backed saddles with Velcro strips on the fenders make it safe for kids with special needs to become skilled equestrians and thus learn to work with their own handicaps as they never have been able to do before!

A Word about Horse Whispering

If you are constantly reading about horses and know a lot about them, you probably have heard of horse whispering, something that many horse behaviorists do today to train horses. This training process is much different than what the majority of horsemen did several decades ago.

We've all read Wild West stories or seen movies in which the cowpoke "broke" a wild horse by climbing on his back and hanging on while the poor horse bucked until he was so exhausted he could hardly stand. What that type of training did was break the horse's spirit, and the horse learned to obey out of fear. Many "bronco busters" from the past also used whips, ropes, sharp spurs, and painful bits to make the horses respond, which they did only to avoid the pain the trainers caused.

Thankfully, the way many horses become reliable mounts has changed dramatically. Today many horses are trained, not broken. The trainer "communicates" with the horse using herd language. Thus, the horse bonds with his trainer quickly, looks to that person as his herd leader, and is ready to obey every command.

Thanks to Monty Roberts, the "man who listens to horses," and other professional horse whispering trainers like him, most raw or green horses (those that are just learning to respond to tack and a rider) are no longer broken.

Horses are now trained to accept the tack and rider in a short time with proven methods of horse whispering. Usually working in a round pen, the trainer begins by making large movements and noise as a predator would, encouraging the horse to run away. The trainer then gives the horse the choice to flee or bond. Through body language, the trainer asks the horse, "Will you choose me to be your herd leader and follow me?"

Often the horse responds with predictable herd behavior by twitching an ear toward his trainer then by lowering his head and licking to display an element of trust. The trainer mocks the horse's passive body language, turns his back on the horse, and, without eye contact, invites him to come closer. The bonding occurs when the horse chooses to be with the human and walks toward the trainer, thus accepting his leadership and protection.

Horse whispering has become one of the most acceptable, reliable, and humane ways to train horses. Today we have multitudes of rider-and-horse teams that have bonded in such a special way, both the rider and the horse enjoy each other's company. So when you're talking to your friends about horses, always remember to say the horses have been trained, not broken. The word *broken* is part of the horse's past and should remain there forever.

Bible Verses about Horses

Do you know there are about 150 verses in the Bible that include the word *horse*? It seems to me that if God mentioned horses so many times in the Bible, then he is very fond of one of his most beautiful creatures.

Some special verses about horses in the Bible make any horse lover want to shout. Look at this exciting passage from the book of Revelation that tells us about a wonderful time in the future:

"I saw heaven standing open and there before me was a white horse, whose rider is called Faithful and True. With justice he judges and makes war. His eyes are like blazing fire, and on his head are many crowns. He has a name written on him that no one knows but he himself. He is dressed in a robe dipped in blood, and his name is the Word of God. The armies of heaven were following him riding on white horses and dressed in fine linen, white and clean" (Revelation 19:11–14).

The rider who is faithful and true is the Lord Jesus Christ. The armies of heaven on white horses who follow Jesus are those who have accepted him as their Lord and Savior. I've accepted Christ, so I know that some day I'll get to ride a white horse in heaven. Do you think he will be a Lipizzaner, an Andalusian, or an Arabian? Maybe it will be a special new breed of white horses that God is preparing just for that special time.

Perhaps you never realized that there are horses in heaven. Perhaps you never thought about how you could go to heaven when you die. You can try to be as good as gold, but the Bible says that to go to heaven, you must ask Jesus to forgive your sins. Verses to think about: "For all have sinned and fall short of the glory of God" (Romans 3:23); "For God so loved the world that he gave his one and only son, that whoever believes in him shall not perish but have eternal life (John 3:16); "For everyone who calls on the name of the Lord will be saved" (Romans 10:13).

Do you want to be part of Jesus' cavalry in heaven some day? Have you ever asked Jesus to forgive your sins and make you ready for heaven? If you've never done so, please ask Jesus to save your soul today.

As I'm riding my prancing white steed with his long wavy mane and tail dragging to the ground, I'll be looking for you!

Glossary of Gaits

Gait–A gait is the manner of movement; the way a horse goes.

There are four natural or major gaits most horses use: walk, trot, canter, and gallop.

Walk–In the walk, the slowest gait, hooves strike the ground in a four-beat order: right hind hoof, right fore (or front) hoof, left hind hoof, left fore hoof.

Trot–In the trot, hooves strike the ground in diagonals in a one-two beat: right hind and left forefeet together, left hind and right forefeet together.

Canter–The canter is a three-beat gait containing an instant during which all four hooves are off the ground. The foreleg that lands last is called the *lead* leg and seems to point in the direction of the canter.

Gallop–The gallop is the fastest gait. If fast enough, it's a four-beat gait, with each hoof landing separately: right hind hoof, left hind hoof just before right fore hoof, left fore hoof.

Other gaits come naturally to certain breeds or are developed through careful breeding.

Running walk–This smooth gait comes naturally to the Tennessee Walking Horse. The horse glides between a walk and a trot.

Pace–A two-beat gait, similar to a trot. But instead of legs pairing in diagonals as in the trot, fore and hind legs on one side move together, giving a swaying action.

Slow gait–Four beats, but with swaying from side to side and a prancing effect. The slow gait is one of the gaits used by five-gaited saddle horses. Some call this pace the *stepping pace* or *amble*.

Amble–A slow, easy gait, much like the pace.

Rack–One of the five gaits of the five-gaited American Saddle Horse, it's a fancy, fast walk. This four-beat gait is faster than the trot and is very hard on the horse.

Jog–A jog is a slow trot, sometimes called a *dogtrot*.

Lope–A slow, easygoing canter, usually referring to a western gait on a horse ridden with loose reins.

Fox trot–An easy gait of short steps in which the horse basically walks in front and trots behind. It's a smooth gait, great for long-distance riding and characteristic of the Missouri Fox Trotter.